TOYS!

AMAZING STORIES
BEHIND SOME GREAT INVENTIONS

DON WULFFSON
ILLUSTRATED BY LAURIE KELLER

SQUARE
FISH

HENRY HOLT AND COMPANY • NEW YORK

SQUARE
FISH

An Imprint of Macmillan
175 Fifth Avenue, New York, NY 10010
mackids.com

Square Fish books may be purchased for business or promotional use.
For information on bulk purchases, please contact the Macmillan Corporate
and Premium Sales Department at (800) 221-7945 x5442 or by e-mail at
specialmarkets@macmillan.com.

Library of Congress Cataloging-in-Publication Data
Wulffson, Don L.
Toys! : amazing stories behind some great inventions / Don Wulffson ;
with illustrations by Laurie Keller.
p.   cm.
Includes bibliographical references.
Summary: Describes the creation of a variety of toys and games,
from seesaws to Silly Putty and toy soldiers to Trivial Pursuit.
ISBN 978-1-250-03409-0 (paperback) / ISBN 978-1-4668-5614-1 (e-book)
1. Toys—History—Juvenile literature.   2. Inventions—History—Juvenile literature.
[1. Toys.   2. Inventions.]   I. Title.
GV1218.5.W85 2000   688.7′2′09—dc21   99-58440

Originally published in the United States by Henry Holt and Company
First Square Fish Edition: 2014
Book designed by Donna Mark
Square Fish logo designed by Filomena Tuosto

3   5   7   9   10   8   6   4   2

AR: 6.8 / LEXILE: 950L

CONTENTS

CONTENTS

*My thanks to Christy Ottaviano and Jane Jordan Browne
for making this book possible; to my wife, Pamela,
for her untiring love and support; to Christian Goodell
for his invaluable research and assistance;
and to Karl Ryden, Patricia Conwell, Kim Kmetz, and
Jeff and Becky Zolot for their contributions to this book.*

For Barbara and Bill
with love

TOYS!

INTRODUCTION

Play-Doh began as a product for cleaning wallpaper. The seesaw was first used as a prop in the bloody spectacle in the arenas of ancient Rome. Long ago there were kites so large that people could be flown on them. Behind every toy there is a story.

But some toys have far stranger stories than others. Only those toys that had the most surprising and unbelievable origins are found in this book.

Even though we know generally where and when a given toy was made, the chapters of this book are not in chronological order because there are all sorts of ways in which toys and their histories overlap. For example, tops have been around much longer than today's action figures—but action figures are a type of doll, and dolls were invented thousands of years before tops. So, really, there is no way to put the history of toys into a simplified order.

In 1976, a time capsule was buried in Washington, D.C. Inside the capsule are dozens of toys from the last century. In 2076, exactly one hundred years later, it will be opened. People then will marvel at the wonderful jumble of toys and see how we lived, how we dressed, and what we believed. Just as we are now, they will be amused and surprised by the toys they find, and from them, try to better understand the past.

THE SLINKY

It was a mistake. A goof-up. An invention that didn't work. A flop; that's what the Slinky was, at least in the beginning.

In 1945, an engineer by the name of Richard James was hard at work in a Philadelphia shipyard. The U.S. Navy had hired him to invent a stabilizing device for its ships. When a ship is plowing through the waves at sea, it pitches and plunges and rocks every which way. And its navigational instruments do, too. Richard's job was to come up with something that would counterbalance the instruments so that they would be level at all times.

Springs. Richard believed that some sort of arrangement of springs would do the trick. He tried all different types and sizes, and put them together in every conceivable way. For weeks he toiled, making dozens of different devices. But none of them worked. In fact, he never did come up with the item the Navy had hired him to invent.

But one day Richard accidentally knocked a large experimental spring off a shelf. It should have just plopped to the floor. Instead, it walked down. Crawled, really. Coil by coil, end over end, it descended onto a stack of books . . . then down to a desktop . . . down to a chair . . . and from there to the floor, where it gathered itself back together.

He tried it again and again. Each time, the same thing happened.

As soon as the workday was over, Richard hurried home. Fascinated with the strange spring, he showed his wife, Betty, what it could do. Together, they tried it out in all sorts of ways and in all sorts of places. It was especially good at walking down stairs.

A toy.

Richard didn't think of it that way. Betty did. She was the one who realized that what her husband had invented was a terrific toy. Betty was also the one who named it.

At first, all sorts of names came to mind, but none seemed quite right. For the next two days she thumbed through a dictionary, keeping a list of some of the best possibilities. Finally, she came upon what she believed was the perfect word to describe the toy: slinky.

Early the next year, Betty and Richard James borrowed $500 to have four hundred Slinkys made. They went from store to store, trying to get the owners to stock them. A few did. But despite Slinky's wonderful ability to walk, it didn't move off the shelves. Not a single one was bought.

Richard and Betty were discouraged but not about to give up. Slinky was a supertoy, they were sure. And it would sell—but people needed to be shown what it could do.

They went to the manager of a large department store named Gimbel's. It took a lot of talking—even a little begging!—but finally they convinced the manager to let them put on a demonstration. Fearing the worst, Richard slipped a dollar to a friend to make sure at least one Slinky would be sold. It turned out, though, that he had no need to worry. Shoppers stared in amazement as the steel coil gracefully walked down a sloped board. Within ninety minutes, the entire stock of four hundred had been sold.

Before long, Richard and Betty were able to start their own company. Within a few years, they were millionaires. As for Slinky, more than 352 million have been sold to date; Slinky's sales are as strong today as ever. In the world of toys, Slinky still walks that walk—and shows no sign of slowing down.

○ The early Slinkys were made of blue-black Swedish steel. In the first year of production, this material was replaced with less expensive American metal.

○ The first Slinkys sold for $1 apiece.

○ There are about eighty feet of wire in a standard-size Slinky.

○ During the Vietnam War (early 1960s–1975) the Slinky reverted to its original role. First intended for the military, Slinky the toy ended up on the battle-field. Carried by radiomen in the jungles of Vietnam, Slinkys were tossed over high tree branches as makeshift antennas.

○ Richard opened a shop in Clifton Heights, Pennsylvania, after developing a machine that could produce a new Slinky every few seconds.

In 1960, Richard became an evangelical missionary in Bolivia.

Slinkys make good scarecrows. After seeds have been planted, try hanging a Slinky on a nearby branch. With the slightest breeze, it'll dance around, and birds will stay away.

Perhaps Slinky's greatest accomplishment was in outer space. Bunches have gone aboard space shuttles. The purpose: to test the effects of zero gravity on springs.

There are now plastic Slinkys, colored ones, those that look like walking rainbows, and others that light up. And then there's Slinky Dog, the classic pull toy; Susie, the Slinky worm; and Loco, a Slinky train.

SEESAW

Some inventions popped up in different parts of the world at different times—but nobody knows for sure where and when they first originated. One of these is the seesaw. The Polynesians, Egyptians, Germans, Greeks, and Chinese all had versions of the seesaw (or teeter-totter, as it is also called).

The Romans were the first, however, to set down any written record of them. See-saws, it seems, were used in ancient Roman circuses—which had very violent exhibitions. Boxing matches to the death, crucifixions, military battles in which the soldiers actually killed each other— these were all part of the Roman circus events. Almost

every act was brutal, and that goes for their seesaw act as well.

Here's how it worked. In the middle of the arena a large seesaw was set up; at either end of the device was a basket big enough to hold a man. Two clowns were then shoved out into the arena. As fast as they could, they ran to the seesaw and hopped into the baskets— just as a lion was set free from a cage. The lion, which hadn't been fed for days, charged the seesaw. When it came toward one of the clowns, he would push off the ground and up into the air. Then the animal would race toward the other clown in the basket on the ground. And that clown would immediately push off and shoot up, out of reach of the ravenous lion. Up and down they would go. The spectators thought this was great fun. For the clowns, however, it wasn't fun at all. Eventually, they began to tire. One would sadly end up as a basket of food for the lion.

The next time you're on a seesaw, you might want to think about how it was once used. And be glad you're just clowning around—and not a clown in the seesaw act at a Roman circus!

- The longest that two people have seesawed is 820 hours. The record was set by Charles Ryan and Philip Duiett of Theodore High School, Theodore, Alabama, February 23 through March 28, 1976.
- The original meaning of the word *seesaw* was "back and forth."
- The original meaning of the word *clown* was "peasant."
- Today, there are seesaws that not only go up and down but swivel in a 360-degree circle.

LEGO

The Great Depression of 1929 put people out of work all over the world. One such person was Ole Kirk Christiansen, who lived in the little town of Billund, Denmark. Mr. Christiansen was a carpenter, but unfortunately there was little work to be found. By 1932, he still did not have a steady job. To make ends meet, Christiansen began handcrafting such things as wooden ironing boards, stepladders, wheelbarrows, and toys. Then, with his wife and son, he would travel the countryside to sell his products to local farmers.

When the Depression finally started to ease up, most people returned to their old jobs. But Christiansen had become very skilled at crafting wooden toys, especially animal pull toys, and there was great demand for them. He realized that he could make more money creating toys than he could building houses. Besides, he enjoyed the work more.

Having decided to go into the toy business full-time, Christiansen opened his own company. He combined two Danish words, *leg godt*, which means "play well," in naming his new company Lego. (Christiansen may not have known it, but *lego* is also a Latin word—and one with a very appropriate meaning. In Latin, *lego* means "I put together.")

When the Lego company opened its doors for business in 1932, no Legos were made there—for the simple reason that they hadn't been invented yet. At first, Christiansen and his employees made only wooden toys

such as dolls, blocks, hobbyhorses, and marionettes. After a year of operation, they began making plastic toys as well.

One day Christiansen whittled some clever new building blocks. What made them unique was that they interlocked. Kids would really like the blocks, he felt sure; but he knew it would be both difficult and expensive to mass-produce wooden ones. Right away, he realized the blocks could be produced much faster and cheaper using plastic instead of wood. In 1949, Christiansen came out with what he called Automatic Binding Bricks. The sets were in two colors: red and white. As they do today, the blocks had studs on top, were hollow underneath, and could be easily stacked and locked together.

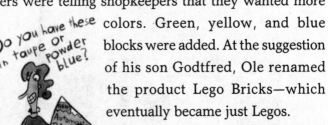

In Europe, the toy was a hit from the get-go. Soon, buyers were telling shopkeepers that they wanted more colors. Green, yellow, and blue blocks were added. At the suggestion of his son Godtfred, Ole renamed the product Lego Bricks—which eventually became just Legos.

Do you have these in taupe or powder blue?

Five years later, Ole and Godtfred improved their product. Tubes were added, which gave kids many

cool, huh?

new and interesting ways to connect the blocks. In the original 1949 version, the bricks could only be stacked directly on top of one another. Now, two eight-studded bricks could be joined in twenty-four different ways. Six eight-studded bricks could be combined in over a *million* ways!

By the end of the 1950s, Legos had become one of the most popular toys in Europe. But not until 1961 did the toy finally reach the United States. Why it took so long for the product to reach this country, no one really knows, but by the early 1970s it was one of the best-loved and bestselling items in America, too.

Presently, Legos are manufactured in hundreds of different sets. Some sets just contain the basics: building blocks and connecting tubes. Others come complete with a wide variety of items for play, such as small cars, roadways, ramps, roofs, and even "city maps." It's a whole little world unto itself, and—perhaps best of all—it's a world that you create.

- Legos are made of a plastic called ABS (acrylonitrile butadiene styrene). During the manufacturing process, the plastic is heated to the consistency of bread dough. It is then pressed into molds, cooled, and ejected— all in about ten seconds.

- The process for making Legos is now almost mistake-free. Out of every million Legos made, an average of only twenty-six are rejected.

- Today, the Lego company produces over 4,200 different-shaped bricks, and they come in almost every color imaginable.

- Legoland Parks and Discovery Centers, designed for kids eleven and under, are located in Billund, Denmark; Carlsbad, California; Chicago, Illinois; and other cities around the world. Most attractions are made of real glued-together Legos from standard kits. The rides are painted and designed to look like they are made out of Legos.

- Between 1949 and 2014, more than 573 billion Lego building bricks were produced.

- In 1969, the first official Lego World Cup building championship was held in Billund with thirty-eight children from fourteen different countries participating.

TOPS

People have been doing it for thousands of years, and they haven't tired of it yet—spinning tops.

The oldest tops were discovered in Babylonia in the nineteenth century. On expeditions in the Middle East, archaeologists opened three-thousand-year-old coffins. Inside were human remains, and with the remains were hand-made objects of every kind, possessions the person most enjoyed in life. The children were buried with their favorite toys. For many, these included tops. The tops were made of clay, either solid or hollow. Etched and painted on the sides were pictures, usually of animals.

From Babylonia, tops made their way to many other countries such as Greece, India, and Russia. But it was in Japan that the art of top making blossomed. The ancient Japanese painted tops with clever designs so that, when they were spun, all sorts of wild, intricate images appeared. The Japanese were the first to put holes in clay tops, which made them hum and whistle as they whirled. Another Japanese innovation was putting tiny lanterns in tops. Spinning in the dark of night, the tops filled a room with lights and shadows that danced across the walls.

The Maori, the original people of New Zealand, invented a top called a *potaka*. These tops, often beautifully inlaid with shells, were pointed at both ends and spun with the flick of a whip. The Maori were so skilled that they could use the whip to stop the top and then set it spinning in reverse. Another Maori top was the *potaka takiri*, which made a screaming, wailing sound when spun. These noisy tops had two special uses. Dozens were sent spinning at funerals, sounding like the whole world was crying for the person who had died. Maori warriors also used them when going into battle. Before they attacked, their *potaka takiri* were set into motion; the screaming and howling unnerved the enemy, and sent a clear warning: "You are in great danger!"

Perhaps the most unusual tops were those used in Europe in the Middle Ages. In many villages there was a single enormous wooden top about the size of a person. Sometimes—especially on icy cold mornings—a group

of villagers would come together and set the top spinning by slapping the sides with their hands. Why? For one thing, the physical exertion helped everybody warm up. Besides, it was good fun and a great way to start the day.

- *Top* comes from a Dutch word meaning "to whirl."
- The gyroscope, a type of top invented in 1810, is used to keep ships and planes level while moving.
- Tops—especially gyroscopes—help scientists better understand the rotation of the earth.
- When dice were outlawed for a time in Rome, people used numbered, six-sided tops instead.
- Playing with a four-sided top called a dreidel is a Hanukkah tradition. Each side has a Hebrew letter, and the letter on which the dreidel falls determines if the player wins a prize.

MR. POTATO HEAD

Straw wrappers *poofed* into orbit. Black olives on the ends of little fingers. Green peas flicked across the table.

As a parent, George Lerner had seen every trick, every stunt, every possible way a child can play with food. And there didn't seem to be any hope of stopping the antics. Begging, yelling, scolding, reasoning, punishing; so far, nothing had worked.

Then it happened.

One night, right in the middle of meal-time monkey business, George suddenly had an idea. Instead of trying to get his kids to stop playing with their food, he'd play with his, too! Only he'd do it in a more civilized way.

After gathering bits of junk from around the house, George grabbed a few potatoes and joined his kids at the table. Into a potato went two bottle caps for eyes. A row of thumbtacks made a metal mouth. And a strawberry on a toothpick made a silly, clownlike nose.

Bingo! Just like that, George went from the grumpy old spoiler of table-time fun to the leader of the gang.

In 1950, George was a model maker at a toy-manufacturing company. After his brainstorm, he started molding all kinds of plastic doodads—eyes, ears, noses, hats, mouths, and mustaches. With sharp little prongs in back, they could be stuck into different kinds of fruits and vegetables (potatoes being the best) to create funny faces.

Over and over, George Lerner tried to sell his Funny Faces for Food kit to toy companies. None of them were interested.

More than two years passed before a breakfast food company bought George's idea. Their plan was to make little packages of the Funny Faces pieces and give them

away as premiums in cereal boxes. George signed a contract selling his idea for $5,000.

At first, George thought he had made a good deal. But then several months later he got a phone call from the owners of Hasbro Industries, a toy company that specialized in making play doctor's and nurse's kits. The owners, Henry Hassenfeld and his son Merrill, had seen the Funny Faces cereal box premium, and they wanted to talk with George.

Henry and Merrill Hassenfeld told George how much they liked his idea. They explained that the company wanted to expand its product line and that his toy was just the sort of thing they were looking for. They wanted to buy the idea and form a partnership with George.

But there was one problem—a *big* problem. George explained that he had sold all the rights to the cereal company.

Henry moaned. Merrill groaned. But the father-son team didn't let the matter drop. They contacted the cereal company and made them a terrific offer: George would give back the $5,000, and the Hasbro company would add another $2,000. An agreement was quickly reached. For a total sum of $7,000, the cereal company sold the rights to George Lerner, who then went into partnership with Merrill and Henry Hassenfeld.

George went on to become a millionaire, and so did the Hassenfelds. When Mr. Potato Head first hit the market in 1952, the toy consisted of hands, feet, eyes, and some smaller details. Parents had to provide the body—a real potato. In 1964, he went plastic. Why? First, because the pieces for the potato were sharp and potentially dangerous. Second, people objected to wasting food.

Mr. Potato Head soon became a family man. First Mrs. Potato Head came into his life, and then eventually daughter Yam and son Spud. For the most part, they're a very happy family—except sometimes the kids play with their food!

- Mr. Potato Head was the first toy ever advertised on television.
- Face parts are now five times larger than the originals made by George Lerner.
- In 1987, Mr. Potato Head's pipe was taken away from him, and a big deal was made over "his" decision to quit. At a ceremony at the White House, his pipe was handed over to the surgeon general of the United States.
- Today there is Fire Rescue Mr. Potato Head, Police Officer Sergeant Starch, Mr. Party Spud, Darth Tater, and a host of other characters.

PLAYING CARDS

Pick up a deck of cards and ask yourself a few questions, such as: Who invented cards? What were the first ones like? And why are there fifty-two in a deck?

Now, pick a card, any card.

Maybe you picked a jack of clubs. What does the jack represent? Do the clubs stand for anything? Read on.

The Chinese invented playing cards about a thousand years ago. There were two types, and they were extremely different from each other. One kind was round, and had various numbers of dots on them; basically, they were paper dice and used for gambling. The other kind was rectangular, and looked like paper money. A game was played with the rectangular deck in which the objective was to end up with the largest amount of paper money.

Cards reached Europe during the thirteenth century, about two hundred years after their invention by the Chinese. In Europe, they were called tarots. European tarot decks contained seventy-eight cards. In time, the tarots, all of which were face cards, came to be used only for fortune-telling. For playing games, a new deck was devised. The number of cards was reduced to fifty-two, symbolic of the number of weeks in a year. Four suits were created (hearts, clubs, diamonds, and spades) to represent the four seasons.

You will make a fortune by growing the world's largest tomatoes.

The first face cards—cards with pictures of royalty on them—came into being in the year 1450. The king was the highest of the face cards, followed by the queen. Next came the jack, the symbolic servant of the royal couple.

During the French Revolution in the eighteenth century, the king and queen of France were overthrown. With the royal family eliminated, some people felt they should disappear from cards, too. Card makers began experimenting with new types of face cards. Pictures of famous people were tried, as were pictures of the gods and goddesses of Greek mythology. But none of the new face cards ever caught on. In time, everyone went back to the royal decks.

Cards of today are two-headed—which makes them right-side-up whichever way they're turned. It hasn't always been that way. Two-headed cards were not invented until 1850, and it was not until after 1870 that this design became standard.

For hundreds of years, the backs of cards were blank. Why? Those who used cards for gambling were afraid of being cheated. Plain white backs, they believed, were harder to mark. Not until 1850 did decorative back designs come into use.

The first educational cards appeared in 1508. When Louis XIV of France (1638–1715) was young, he learned geography, history, and other subjects using educational decks. The lessons were printed on one side of the card, leaving the other for game playing.

I thought it was shaped like a banana.

Fact: The earth is round.

The popularity of cards and card playing has grown tremendously since the invention of cards by the Chinese. In the United States, more than a hundred million decks of cards are sold every year. And with just one pack of ordinary cards, more than a thousand different games can be played.

- Throughout history, cards have been made from many unusual materials. There have been silver cards, leather cards, and even rubber cards—for playing games in the water.
- When Russia was a communist country, communist

leaders such as Stalin, Marx, and Lenin were pictured on face cards.

The Puritans called playing cards "the devil's picture book," and believed it was sinful to have cards in the house.

The earliest European cards were hand-painted and far too costly for most people. But in the fifteenth century, wood engraving was invented, which found its principal use in the printing of playing cards. This made cards affordable to almost everyone.

Playing cards are taxed in almost every country. In the United States, they have been taxed since 1894.

SILLY PUTTY

In 1942, during World War II, the United States was experiencing a severe shortage of natural rubber. A synthetic form was desperately needed for the production of gas masks, boots, and tires. The military turned to the General Electric Company for an answer.

At the company's lab in New Haven, Connecticut, James Wright went to work on the project. He tried every chemical combination he could think of. But nothing produced the effect he needed until he mixed boric acid and silicone oil. Together, the substances became a soft, rubbery compound.

Excited, Wright began experimenting with his creation. He discovered that when tossed on the floor, the plastic putty didn't just bounce—it bounced better and higher than rubber. It also stretched farther, didn't decay, withstood extreme cold without cracking, and could take the highest temperatures without melting. And craziest of all was its ability to lift words and images off the pages of newspapers and comic books.

Great stuff. Absolutely fantastic, in fact. Almost anything could be done with it—except the one thing it was supposed to do: serve as a substitute for rubber. It simply didn't get hard enough.

Nutty Putty. Bouncing Putty. Bouncing Blubber. Around the General Electric lab, the curious compound picked up all sorts of names. And it became

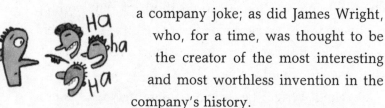

a company joke; as did James Wright, who, for a time, was thought to be the creator of the most interesting and most worthless invention in the company's history.

Years passed, the war ended, and Wright's fascinating flop was all but forgotten. But one day his boss surprised him by suggesting that there must be some sort of use for the strange putty he had created.

An informal contest was held. All the engineers at the lab were given a shot at figuring out a practical purpose for the substance. Not one decent idea was offered. Nevertheless, James and his boss kept at it. Whenever visitors came by the lab, a demonstration was put on— and the question put forward as to what the putty might be used for. The query was always greeted with silence.

Still unwilling to accept failure, the company made one last try; samples were mailed to several of the world's top scientists, challenging them to figure out a practical application for Bouncing Putty (as it was then commonly known).

Same result. It seemed even the best scientists in the world couldn't come up with a worthwhile use for the substance.

One evening in 1948 an engineer from General Electric went to a party. Coming straight from work, he happened 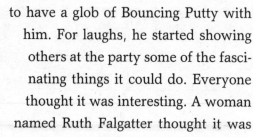 to have a glob of Bouncing Putty with him. For laughs, he started showing others at the party some of the fascinating things it could do. Everyone thought it was interesting. A woman named Ruth Falgatter thought it was more than interesting: it was a toy!

Finally, someone had seen the putty for what it was, for what it had really been all along—a silly novelty that was as intriguing to adults as it was to kids. Not surprisingly, Ruth Falgatter was a toy-store owner. Accompanying her at the party was Peter Hodgson, a friend who helped her write sales and advertising material for her shop.

A few days later, Peter and Ruth met to put together her holiday catalogue. After talking it over, they decided to include Bouncing Putty on a page spotlighting gifts for adults. The ad read: "Do a thousand nutty things with *Bouncing Putty*. Comes in a handy clear plastic case. A guaranteed hoot at parties! Price: Only $2.00!"

Surprisingly enough, Bouncing Putty sold better than almost everything else in the catalogue. Ruth continued stocking the product in her store, but she had no interest in manufacturing and marketing it. But Peter Hodgson did. It so happened that he was over $12,000 in debt; the crazy new product might be just the thing to turn his fortunes around. He made an agreement with General Electric, and then with borrowed money ($147), bought a lot of Bouncing Putty from the company. With his last few dollars, he hired students from Yale University to separate it into one-ounce balls and package it in plastic

eggs. Because "bouncing" described only one of the many different things the substance could do, Hodgson changed the name to something catchier—Silly Putty.

With high hopes and boxes full of Silly Putty eggs, Hodgson headed off to the 1950 New York Toy Fair. Hardly anyone paid Peter and his putty any attention. He was ready to pack it in when he worked out a contract with Doubleday Bookstores. Doubleday planned to carry Silly Putty in their stores.

A few months later a writer for *The New Yorker* bought some Silly Putty at one of the bookseller's outlets in Manhattan. He was so excited by its strange properties that he took it to work with him the next day, plunked it down next to his typewriter, and wrote a column about Silly Putty for the magazine. Incredibly, within three days, orders for Silly Putty had topped a quarter of a million—with more coming in by the minute.

Just like that, James Wright and Peter Hodgson became a success story. As for Silly Putty, it was soon all over America. Children (and a lot of adults) played with Silly Putty—the substance that had bombed so badly for the military only to bounce back as a bestselling toy.

Silly Putty has hardly changed since it was first invented, but the process used to print color comics has. The result: Silly Putty no longer does a very good job lifting images off the pages of the Sunday funnies.

- Silly Putty was originally only available in peachy pink. During the 1960s, other colors were offered. Fluorescent shades of Silly Putty were added in 1990, with a glow-in-the-dark version introduced the following year.
- Ironically, after becoming a popular toy, many practical uses have been found for Silly Putty. Mechanics use it to clean equipment, dry cleaners to remove lint, and zookeepers to make casts of animal footprints for purposes of identification.

WINDUP TOYS AND AUTOMATONS

What makes a windup toy work?

Turning a key tightens a spring inside the toy. As the spring unwinds, it turns gears, which move the toy's parts.

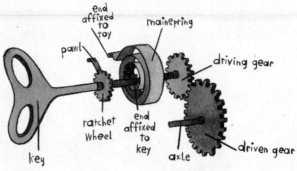

Today's windup toys are for children, and most of them are relatively simple. Originally, windup toys were for adults—usually royalty—and were often extremely complicated and expensive. Rather than windup toys, they were called automatons and usually featured people, animals, or vehicles of some kind. With the finest crafts-manship, automatons moved by means of elaborate internal clockwork devices; their exterior was formed and decorated by hand, in many cases with the utmost skill and attention to detail.

In the late 1400s, a German inventor by the name of Karel Grod was often invited to royal banquets. Sitting at the table, Grod would open his hand and release a metal fly that buzzed across the room, circled the long dining table, and then returned to rest on its maker's hand. A few years later, Grod created a life-size mechanical eagle that could fly around town and then return to its original spot.

In 1509, the famous artist and inventor Leonardo da Vinci constructed a mechanical lion to welcome Louis XII to Italy. When the French king was seated on his throne, Leonardo placed the animal on the floor at the opposite end of a great hall. As spectators stared in amazement, the clockwork lion moved slowly toward

the king. It stopped in front of him, and, as if in tribute to the king, tore open its chest with its claws. A decorative fleur-de-lis, the symbol of French royalty, tumbled out and fell at the king's feet.

An even more incredible story is told about René Descartes, a renowned French philosopher and scientist of the 1600s. Descartes believed that all living creatures, including people, are basically just highly developed machines. To demonstrate this he constructed a life-size mechanical girl. Shortly after completing the automaton, whom he called Franchina, he took her on a sea voyage. By accident, the captain of the ship set her in motion. Terrified by her sudden movement, the captain ran. The robotic Franchina kept coming toward him. In a panic, the captain grabbed the automaton and threw it overboard.

Perhaps the most fantastic mechanical figures of all time were created by Jean-Pierre Droz, a Swiss watchmaker, and by his son Henri-Louis. One of those made by Jean-Pierre, called the Writer, was a full-size likeness

of a young boy seated at a desk. When put into motion, the clockwork child dipped his pen in a bottle of ink, shook off the surplus with a flick of the wrist, then proceeded to write clear and correct sentences. As each line was completed, the hand holding the pen moved to the beginning of the next line.

Superior to the Writer was the Designer, an automaton created by Jean-Pierre's son Henri-Louis. Like an artist studying his model, the automaton paused from time to time as he sketched, examined his work, corrected errors, and even blew the eraser dust from the paper. On one occasion, the Designer was seated before King Louis XVI of France; after working for some time, the automaton put down his pencil and gestured with his hand to his work: a portrait of the French king. Later,

Handsome devil, aren't I?

when Henri-Louis gave a demonstration in England, his automaton drew portraits of the English monarch and other royalty.

Henri-Louis died at the height of his fame, in 1790. With him, the art of making automatons declined. Though a few choice pieces were created after this time by other artists, the quality of work went steadily down-hill. More and more, the toys were made by machine rather than hand, and they became generally much simpler and cheaper. By the nineteenth century, they were made of tin or plastic, and mass-produced in large numbers.

Today, windup cars, tractors, trains, spaceships, and robots roll off assembly lines by the thousands. Many of them are clever and fun to play with, but the era of automatons is over. Will this specialized art form return? What do you think?

○ Before the Christian era, the Greeks and Arabs made mechanical toys powered by air, water, or mercury.

○ Makers of early windup toys were sometimes accused of sorcery because their creations seemed miraculous.

○ King Louis XIV, Napoleon, and Queen Victoria all collected windup toys.

○ Empress Josephine of France, wife of Napoleon, loved giving automatons to children, especially the poor.

HOBBYHORSES

In the fifteenth century, an unknown German artist did a very unusual painting. The work, *Saint Dorothy and the Christ Child*, shows Jesus as a child happily riding a hobby-horse. Though the painting was beautifully rendered, Christian clergymen criticized both the painting and the artist. They called the artist a sinner and a fool. Jesus could not have ridden a hobbyhorse since it had not yet been invented when he was a boy.

The artist apologized for creating the painting. He told the clergymen that they were right about the toy not existing then and that it was careless of him to have painted such a picture.

As punishment, the clergymen ordered the artist never to paint again.

Almost four hundred years passed. In the nineteenth century archaeologists on a dig in the Middle East discovered many hobbyhorses—most of which were between one thousand and three thousand years old. Incredibly, hobbyhorses *had* been around during the time that Jesus had lived, and were definitely one of the toys he might have played with as a child.

The painter never knew he had been right. He ended his career believing his painting was both sinful and inaccurate.

The hobbyhorse was invented in the Middle East, in and around where Christ grew up. It was also invented in China, Europe, and Africa. Like so many inventions, this toy sprang up in many parts of the world.

There are three kinds of hobbyhorses: the stick variety, the rocking horse, and the wheeled hobbyhorse.

The stick or broom handle horse has remained popular for centuries. Some of the early versions were rather crudely made, but they served their purpose. As an old English nursery rhyme put it:

> *I had a little hobbyhorse*
> *And it was dapple gray.*
> *Its head was made of pea-straw*
> *Its tail was made of hay.*

During the Middle Ages, such stick horses were sold at summer fairs in Europe, and every toy seller carried them in his pack. They came in various sizes; and sometimes the sticks were long enough for several children to ride at the same time.

The rocking horse evolved from the rocking baby cradle (which later was the inspiration for the rocking chair). As tin and iron became popular in toy making in the nineteenth century, all sorts of new rocking toys were invented. Toy makers introduced mechanical horses, coaches, buggies, fire engines, and every kind of vehicle a horse could pull. Other animals also entered the picture: rocking lions, zebras, elephants, and tigers. Such toys are still popular today.

Hobbyhorses on wheels are the most recent variation. However, they are not as new as was previously believed. It was once thought that the first wheeled hobbyhorse was made in England during the seventeenth century. It

Hobbyhorses

stick-type horse

rocking horse

Why aren't there any rocking worms?!

wheeled hobbyhorse

yeeeha!

I don't want to spoil his party, but I had one of those 300 years ago!

was later discovered that children were riding around on them in China at least three hundred years earlier. The proof is a huge silk wall hanging woven in fourteenth-century China that shows children riding on hobbyhorses with wooden wheels.

Hobbyhorse history is fun and often filled with surprises. As for the future, we can only wonder what it holds for this toy that has been a part of our lives for so long. Will they be solar-powered, or trainlike and run on tracks, or will there be robotic hobbyhorses? No one knows. All we can be sure of is that they will be around for a very long time!

- Nawbrama, an African king of the nineteenth century, always rode on a wheeled hobbyhorse pushed by slaves.

- In the epic poem the *Iliad*, the Greeks built what might be considered the largest, most unusual, and most clever hobbyhorse of all time—the Trojan Horse.

- During the Middle Ages, actors and dancers sometimes had hobbyhorses attached to their costumes in such a way that it appeared they were riding them. The hobbyhorses were either sewn to the costume or slung from a belt.

- In Europe during the Middle Ages, a "hobby" was a high-spirited, medium-size breed of horse.

BICYCLES

In the world of inventions, the bicycle followed right after the wheeled hobbyhorse. All in all, the bicycle actually evolved from the kiddy-car. It had four wheels and could be moved only by pushing with the feet against the ground. Often the kiddy-cars were made to resemble animals.

More speed!

Children wanted their kiddy-cars to go faster. First, the animal design was done away with. Then off went a couple of the wheels. The two remaining wheels were greatly enlarged and then aligned down the center of the vehicle. Finally, handlebars and footrests were added.

These primitive two-wheelers went much faster than the four-wheeled kiddy-cars. They were a huge improvement, but they had a long way to go before becoming

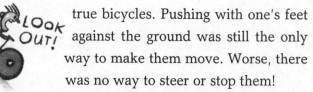

LOOK OUT! true bicycles. Pushing with one's feet against the ground was still the only way to make them move. Worse, there was no way to steer or stop them!

In 1816, Frenchman J. Niepce invented the first bicycle that could be steered. Called a *céléripède*, the contraption, including the wheels, was made entirely of wood.

In 1839, a Scottish blacksmith by the name of Kirkpatrick Macmillan came up with the idea of putting pedals on bicycles. The pedals were connected by long rods to the rear wheel; and the rear wheel was made to turn by pushing back and forth on the pedals. Though Macmillan's bicycle was constructed mostly of wood, the rods and pedals were iron, and the wooden wheels had iron tires.

How much did Macmillan know about the history of the bicycle? Chances are he was well aware that it had evolved from the hobbyhorse. A finishing touch he put on the front of his bicycle was a carved wood horse's head.

Good bikey.

It was a teenage French boy and his father who invented pedals that work like those we use today—pedals that go around in a continuous motion instead of being pushed back and forth. The way they came up with the idea is fascinating; it's one of those cases in which the basic idea behind one invention led to the idea for another.

Here's what happened.

One afternoon in March 1861, Ernest Michaux and his father, Pierre, set out to make footrests for a bicycle. His gaze coming to rest on a grindstone in the shed, young Ernest suddenly exclaimed that he had an idea. They could put pedals on the bicycle that, like the pedals on a grindstone, could be kept turning in a nonstop motion.

For several days the two worked side by side. When the bicycle was finished, Ernest took the first ride. Later he wrote: "I was elated. The drive-wheel revolved as though turning the handle and crank of a grindstone. The bicycle worked beautifully."

Before the year was out, the Michaux were manufacturing and selling their new bicycles, which they called *vélocipèdes*. The name is French, and means "speedy feet."

A man named James Starley invented spoked wheels and tubular steel frames. He also invented the world's goofiest-looking bicycle—the kind with a huge front wheel and a tiny rear wheel. Called the *ordinary* (for no known reason), it had both its good and bad points.

The ordinary gave a much faster ride than any bicycle before it. Its speed was partly due to its hollow, light frame, but even more so because of its giant front drive wheel. Bicycles at this time had no gears; the speed at which they moved depended entirely on the drive wheel. The larger the wheel, the faster the bike.

The ordinary was not only fast, it gave a smooth ride. Enthusiasts liked it for the same reason that most people hated it: riding an ordinary was dangerous, tricky, and required great skill.

Because of its height it was difficult just to mount the bike, and because of the size of its drive wheel it was also hard to get the vehicle going. It was tricky to steer, too, and it tipped over easily, especially when turning. Worst of all, any attempt at braking, particularly when headed downhill, often sent the rider flying over the handlebars.

Most people did not—*could not*—ride an ordinary.

It was not fear of falling and getting hurt. The reason was a different problem altogether, and a pretty insurmountable one. Only long-legged people could ride these bicycles; individuals of average build—or less than average—could not reach the pedals! Thus, during this era, most people had to ride tricycles.

Eighteen seventy-four. That was the year that H. J. Lawson designed what he called the *safety* bicycle. Chain-driven, and made with wheels of equal size, the safety was the forerunner of the modern bicycle. Fourteen years later, John Dunlop made the safety a softer ride; he came up with the idea of pneumatic—air-filled—tires. Until this time, they had either been solid rubber or semi-hollow "cushion tires."

In addition to inventing the ordinary, James Starley was determined to make a bicycle for women that was "proper"; that is, one designed so a woman could ride it in formal attire without straddling the seat. What he came up with was definitely the craziest, most danger-ous bicycle ever invented. Imagine trying to ride a bike side-saddle. Starley designed and built a bike that women rode while sitting on a 45-degree angle to the front. The contraption had a boxlike, sideways seat, and was fitted with a complex pedal-and-crank mechanism. Naturally,

Have the bandages ready!

it was almost impossible
to steer and balance; and almost
every woman who tried riding it got hurt.

To this day, we still see a carryover of this idea of spe-cial bikes for females. Take, for example, the down-curved, loop frame on women's bicycles. Back in the nineteenth century, manufacturers made them this way to give clearance for ladies' frocks and dresses. But that was a long time ago. Fortunately, things have changed; and female cyclists now wear pants and shorts!

———

○ Macmillan was not only the first to put pedals on a bicycle, he also committed the first ever biking offense. On June 10, 1842, after a forty-mile ride, he accidentally crashed into a child, and was fined five shillings.

○ Scotsman John Dunlop developed the idea for the pneumatic tire to help his son ride his tricycle to school over rough cobblestones.

○ The highest speed ever achieved on a bicycle was set by Dr. A. Abbott of California in 1980. Pedaling behind a giant windshield mounted on a speeding car, Dr. Abbott reached a speed of 140 miles per hour.

○ In Japan there are contests to see who can go the *slowest* on a bicycle. The record was set in 1965 by T. Mitsuishi of Tokyo, who rode his bike for five hours and twenty-five minutes *without going any-where!*

○ In the nineteenth century, a new type of bicycle became common: the *tandem*, which two people could ride at the same time. Tandem tricycles also came into vogue during this era, especially in England.

○ In 1987, two men rode their bikes to the top of the Himalayas, Mount Kala Pattar, a peak of more than eighteen thousand feet.

○ Quite a few people have accomplished the feat of riding a bicycle across the United States. One was Becky Gorton. Becky was only eleven years old when she arrived in Boston, Massachusetts, on July 22, 1973, having set out from Olympia, Washington, on June 6 of that year.

REMOTE-CONTROLLED TOYS

Believe it or not, remote-controlled toys had their beginnings as weapons of war.

In 1866, Englishman Robert Whitehead was given the job of "development of a means whereby Her Majesty can blow up a ship from a goodly distance from the ship." After several months of work, Whitehead came up with a primitive torpedo: a small boat stuffed with explosives and steered by wires attached to the motor. To test the new device, a rusty old ship was towed into range—in this case, a couple of miles away. All was ready for the big test.

Plan

The Royal Remote Control connected to a small boat carrying explosives. When small boat hits big ship, the big ship BLOWS UP!

Alas, the first torpedo bombed. The torpedo boat blew up before reaching its target.

But all was not lost. In fact, something good came out of this flop. British toy manufacturers, hearing of Whitehead's torpedo boat, made use of the idea. Soon, English children could be seen playing with miniature battery-powered boats steered by wires connected to a simple control system.

During World War I (1914–1918), the Germans more or less reinvented Whitehead's weapon. Motorboats packed with explosives were developed by the German navy to ram enemy ships. Since radio waves rather than wires were used, the boats were the first true remote-controlled devices in history.

Like Whitehead's invention, the German weapon was converted into a toy. In the 1920s, a few radio-controlled toy boats and cars appeared on the market. By the 1950s, there were thousands.

Throughout World War II (1939–1945), the Germans invented all sorts of bizarre weapons. There was the flying tank (an idea that never got off the ground). And the wind cannon—which  was supposed to knock down enemy planes with big blasts of air—another unworkable idea. Strangest of all may have been the Goliath.

The Goliath was a little tank—one so small not even a single person could fit inside. Instead of soldiers, the Goliath carried explosives. The idea was to send the radio-controlled miniature tank in the direction of the enemy. Once it had reached its target, it was detonated by the soldier operating the controls.

Though hundreds of Goliaths were made during the war, not one is reported to have caused much damage. Rarely did these mini-tanks even come close to reaching their targets. Most got stuck in the mud or crashed into an obstacle and flopped over. The rest, as they slowly rumbled along, were shot to pieces and stopped in their tracks.

Remote-controlled miniature airplanes were used by the armies of many countries during World War II. As with torpedo boats and mini-tanks, the small planes were sometimes filled with explosives and guided by a controller toward the enemy. Other remote-controlled planes had cameras mounted on their bellies. As they were flown over hostile territory, the camera snapped reconnaissance photos to spy on the enemy.

Ultimately, remote-controlled miniature planes were not very successful in achieving either of their wartime goals. But after the war, in the 1950s, miniature planes were reconceived as remote-controlled toys.

During the 1960s, and in the following decades, a wide variety of new remote-controlled toys came onto the scene. Robots were the newest addition, with Mr. Atom leading the way. Toy rockets, spaceships, and lunar vehicles soon followed.

How do remote-controlled toys work? Take a look at a remote-controlled toy car, for example.

Inside the car is a battery that provides power for what is called the drive motor. There is a steering motor, steering control arms, and a radio receiver attached to

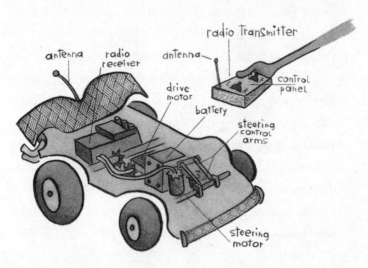

radio transmitter

antenna radio receiver antenna drive motor battery control panel steering control arms steering motor

an antenna. This antenna picks up radio signals from an antenna on the control panel in the user's hands. The control panel is a radio transmitter; signals from it go to the receiver in the car, telling it to speed up or slow down, go backward or forward, left or right.

In many respects, remote-controlled toys are miniaturized versions of cars, planes, and boats.  There is one important difference, however. Though remote-controlled toys are based on weapons technology, they are used for fun, not war.

───

○ Remote-controlled devices that are familiar in many households include garage door openers, televisions, and DVD players.

○ One of the most interesting uses of remote control is found in coal mining. Called a ROLF (remotely operated longwall face), the device directs the operation of a huge machine that cuts coal from the mine and loads it onto a conveyor belt.

○ Police and the military use remote-controlled robotic devices in extremely dangerous situations. These robots can be controlled to disarm or even detonate bombs.

RAGGEDY ANN

Around the turn of the century, John Gruelle was a cartoonist for the *Indianapolis Star*. He had what
most people might consider a very
unusual habit for a grown man—
he always carried a doll wherever
he went. At work, he propped the
doll in a corner of his desk, and at
night he never failed to take it
home with him. None of John's
co-workers at the *Star* made fun
of him; in fact, they never even
asked him about the doll. Everyone
already knew what had happened.

One icy December day in 1914, John's eight-year-old
daughter, Marcella, was playing in the attic at her
grandmother's home. Marcella's eyes suddenly lit up.

In a wooden chest was an old, tattered doll. Some of its hair of red yarn had fallen out. It had no eyes, no nose, no mouth—in fact, it really had no face at all. Even so, Marcella's grandmother recognized the doll immediately. It had belonged to Marcella's mother when she had been a little girl—her absolute favorite, she had completely worn it out.

Right then and there, Marcella adopted the doll as her own. Excited, she quickly bundled up, and with doll in hand, headed off into the snow to the *Star*. Rushing into her father's office, she displayed her wonderful discovery.

John Gruelle was about to tell his daughter that he had a deadline to meet, but Marcella's concern for her newfound doll was simply a far more important matter—her doll needed a new face!

Putting his work aside, John took the doll from his daughter's arms. Carefully, with his pen, the cartoonist drew the basic features— making them happy ones, of course. And making his little girl happy, too.

That night Marcella's mom went to work on the doll. She restuffed it, patched its sparse red hair, sewed on button eyes, and made it a dress with a white apron. As a final touch, she sewed a little red heart on its chest with the words "I love you" written inside.

She's beautiful.

Marcella was delighted with the transformation. But now her doll needed a name. What should she call her?

After thinking a bit, her parents came up with Raggedy Ann. It was a combination of two names. *Raggedy* was from a poem entitled "The Raggedy Man," written by family friend James Whitcomb Riley. *Ann* was borrowed from *Little Orphan Annie,* the title of another poem by Mr. Riley as well as the name of the comic strip by Harold Gray.

Everyone in the Gruelle household fell in love with Raggedy Ann. At bedtime, as Marcella lay snuggled with her doll, John made up fanciful tales about the marvelous adventures of Raggedy Ann. And it was not long before the floppy rag doll began to appear in his comic strip, *Mr. Twee Deedle*. But Raggedy Ann didn't have a starring role. Usually she was just shown dangling from a child's hand.

One day Marcella became ill. As she lay in bed, her doll was always by her side. Her parents were there, too; and her father continued to make up stories about Raggedy Ann. The stories comforted Marcella, and John hoped they would encourage her to get well. But she grew increasingly weak and frail, and soon hardly ever left her bed.

Marcella was only ten years old when she died in 1916—with Raggedy Ann clutched in her arms.

In time, John started writing down the stories he had made up for his little girl. Eventually, dozens of his hand-illustrated Raggedy Ann books were published. He and his wife began handcrafting small quantities of the dolls.

As John would later write: "It was our way of coping with Marcella's death—and to assure that in some way our beautiful little daughter lived on forever."

Indeed she has. The Raggedy Ann books are still popular today, and Raggedy Ann can be seen on television and in stage shows. And, of course, the doll with the red heart graces the bedrooms of millions of children around the world.

- When Mr. and Mrs. Gruelle made their first small quantity of handcrafted dolls, the yarn hair was brown instead of red.
- To this day, every Raggedy Ann doll has a heart. Those made by the Gruelles had a heart-shaped candy imprinted with the words "I Love You."
- The first mass-produced Raggedy Ann dolls contained a cardboard heart under the fabric. Children could feel it by running their fingers across the chest.
- Raggedy Ann has her own newsletter (*Rags*), her own store (The Last Great Company, in Cashiers, North Carolina), and even her own festival, held each year on the weekend before Memorial Day (in Arcola, Illinois, the birthplace of John Gruelle).

TOY SOLDIERS

And sometimes for an hour or so
I watched my leaden soldiers go,
With different uniforms and drills
Among the bedclothes, through the hills.

ROBERT LOUIS STEVENSON

Boys in ancient Greece played with tiny clay gladiators riding in metal carriages pulled by wooden horses. In Europe during the Middle Ages, boys played with wooden knights that had movable parts attached to strings. By having their strings manipulated, the little wooden puppet knights—with swords, spears, and shields—would do battle with each other. Most of the knights were in full armor, and often they were mounted on wheeled horses.

As a child, King Louis XIII of France (1601–1643) played with lead soldiers, which he placed in holes cut into a wooden board. When his son (Louis XIV) was twelve, the king had the largest, most expensive set of toy soldiers made for him. The soldiers were solid silver, and cost the equivalent of $35,000 to make (they are now worth several million dollars). Not to be outdone by his father, when Louis XIV grew up, he had a huge set of windup toy soldiers made in Germany for *his* son. The windup warriors went through all the basic wartime maneuvers. They marched to the left and to the right, doubled their ranks, fired toy guns, lowered their weapons, and then retreated.

Czar Peter II of Russia also had a very large set of toy soldiers made—but for himself, not his children. While the czar never led his troops into battle, he did spend a great deal of his time playing with his toy troops.

Another ruler who was fond of collecting toy soldiers was Decebalus, the king of Dacia (now Romania). He had hundreds of life-size toy soldiers, all dressed in the uniform of the Dacian army.

In A.D. 87, Decebalus received word that a large Roman army was advancing on his capital. Knowing they would be facing a superior force, the Dacian citizens and soldiers expected to be defeated. As the Romans came into view across a distant plain, King Decebalus suddenly had an idea. He ordered his people to lower his army of puppets over the city walls and move them about on the ground below. Viewing the huge army from afar, and not realizing the soldiers were just toys, the Romans concluded that they were greatly outnumbered and quickly retreated.

Throughout history there have been all kinds of toy soldiers made of almost every possible material—gold, silver, lead, wood, ceramic, even papier-mâché and cardboard. Today they are mostly made of plastic or synthetic rubber.

the less popular marshmallow soldier

Eleven and a half inches tall, fully jointed, and with twenty-one moving parts, G.I. Joe captured the toy soldier world in 1962. The idea for the product was based on a TV series, *The Lieutenant.* As for the name of the toy, it came from a World War II movie, *The Story of G.I. Joe.* By 1965, G.I. Joe was the best-selling toy among children five to twelve years old. And not just with boys. Girls also played with Joe. To date, more than ten million G.I. Joes have been sold.

A modern spin-off of toy soldiers are action figures— such as mountain climbers, martial artists, athletes, explorers, and astronauts. Their popularity took off with the release of the first *Star Wars* movie in 1977. Almost overnight, Han Solo, Obi-Wan Kenobi, and Princess Leia action figures were surpassing G.I. Joe in toy sales.

Although action figures are extremely popular, there is still great interest in toy soldiers. But the toy soldier collectors are now almost all adults! Kids usually collect action figures for only a few months. And then along comes the next action figure who, for a time, becomes the "latest and greatest."

- When China's first emperor, Ch'in Shih Huang Ti, died in 210 B.C., he was buried with eight thousand life-size toy soldiers.
- After the American Civil War, toy soldiers were edible since they were made of sugar, chocolate, and flour paste.
- In the 1870s, while England and France were at war, many British bowling alleys featured ninepins shaped like French soldiers.
- In the late nineteenth century in France, more than five million tin soldiers were made from discarded sardine containers.
- Before settling on G.I. Joe, the makers of the toy considered such names as Skip the Navy Frogman, Rocky the Marine Paratrooper, and Ace the Fighter Pilot.
- In 1967, a short-lived Talking G.I. Joe went on the market. When kids yanked on his dog tags, he yelled out eight battlefield commands.

TWISTER

Back in the 1960s, Reyn Guyer and his dad specialized in advertising products for various companies such as Kraft Foods and Pillsbury.

One afternoon in 1965, Reyn was contacted by a Wisconsin shoe polish firm that wanted a clever way to advertise its product. The firm's idea was to create a gift premium that kids would cut out of newspapers, magazines, or comic books. After sending in the premiums plus a dollar to the company, the children would receive a gift in the mail. But what should the gift be?

 Reyn put on his thinking cap. First he thought of colored patches that children could stick to their shoes as decorations. This led to another idea: putting a multicolored, circular design on a life-size board. Each child would have a different color

on his or her feet, and then would have to stretch out—
hands and feet—and extend to that same color else-
where on the board without falling down.

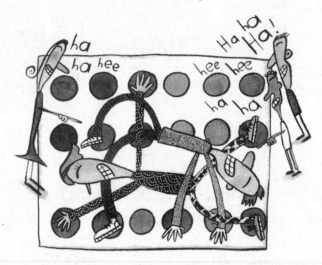

An artist for Reyn's company sketched out the design
on a large piece of plastic. Then Reyn recruited eight
employees to test out his idea. Before long, the players
were all tangled up and howling with laughter. Reyn
realized that he had invented a new game that would
appeal to both kids and adults. Rules were written up
and a spinner dial was added to indicate the color of the
square to which a player had to move on each turn.
After talking it over with his father, Reyn decided to call
the game Pretzel.

The foot patches idea was sold to the shoe polish company. Meanwhile, Reyn presented the game of Pretzel to

the Milton Bradley toy company. They loved it—except for the name, which they changed to Twister.

At first, most store owners were reluctant to stock it. Twister was not exclusively for children or adults; thus, they weren't sure how to advertise it or where to shelve it. And then there was an even bigger problem: how could they explain the game to customers?

The problem was solved literally overnight. On the evening of May 3, 1966, millions of Americans watching *The Tonight Show* saw what this new game was all about. The host then was Johnny Carson, and one of his guests was the celebrity Eva Gabor. For laughs, the two tried out Twister. With the host and his guest crazily entangled,

and the audience tied up in knots laughing, Twister's future was guaranteed. The next day, toy stores were flooded with requests for the game. By year's end, over three million had been sold—more than ten times as many as Milton Bradley had expected. Today, Twister is still the bestselling party game in the United States.

○ A dance craze called "The Twist," which began in 1960 and lasted a few years, added to the popularity of the game. Songs by Chubby Checker, who was known as "Mister Twister," were often played at parties while the game was in full swing.

- According to the president of Milton Bradley, Twister was "the first game in history to turn the human body into a vital component of play."

- Twister was a big hit on college campuses. In 1987, a record-breaking 4,160 contestants tied themselves in knots playing a Twister marathon at the University of Massachusetts.

- For those who like to play Twister in a bathing suit, there is a version called the Water Twister Mat.

PARCHEESI

It would be *very* hard to find a game that has more surprising origins than Parcheesi.

In India during the 1570s, workers in a weaving factory were experimenting with new patterns and designs. Admiring a piece of cloth with an unusual design, one of the weavers came up with the idea that the pattern could be turned into a game.

Hey!

Within a few short years, the game became the most popular in India. At first the game was called Pachisi, which means twenty-five in Hindi, the primary language of India. It was called this because twenty-five was the highest possible throw a person could make with the dice.

Pachisi was popular with both adults and children. When it was played indoors, a piece of cloth with the embroidered Pachisi pattern was used for a game board. Outdoors, the design was drawn on the ground with a

Want to be a token, little guy?

sharp stick. Objects such as spoons, colorful rocks, and small toys served as the tokens. Whether played on cloth or on the ground, the object of the game was the same— to be the first to get one's token in the middle square.

Kings and queens also played Pachisi. Akbar the Great, who ruled India from 1556 to 1605, was obsessively fond of the game. He loved it so much that when he had a palace built for himself, he turned a courtyard into a giant Pachisi board! Very carefully and artistically, workers laid red and white tiles in the proper design amidst a lush flowering garden.

When it was done, Akbar invited other noblemen and women over to his palace for a life-size game of Pachisi. Large dice were made from cowrie shells and primarily attractive young women were used as tokens. When the dice were tossed, the young women would move as many

squares as allowed. The winner, of course, was the first person to maneuver his or her "token" to the middle.

In the nineteenth century, this amusement of Indian royalty was converted into a British board game. From England, it traveled across the Atlantic to America, where its name was changed to Parcheesi.

The next time you play the game, tell your friends and family some of the interesting facts about the way Pachisi came to be and how it was once played. Maybe you will even want to chalk out a life-size board and—like Akbar did centuries ago—use real people as tokens!

- In the United States, Parcheesi was the favorite pastime of inventor Thomas Edison and President Calvin Coolidge.
- Following Akbar's example, other Indian emperors had Pachisi gardens made for themselves. Only one of these—that at the palace in Agra—survives today.
- Parcheesi is the third bestselling game in U.S. history; Monopoly is first, followed by Scrabble.

CHECKERS

Today, checkers is played on a board marked with sixty-four squares of alternating colors (usually black and red). Each contestant has twelve disks, flat pieces called men. The object is to move these pieces diagonally

across the board in such a way as to capture the opponent's men or block their progress. The men can be moved forward only, and only on the black squares. However, if a man reaches the back line on an opponent's side, it is crowned by having a second checker placed on top of it, and becomes a king. A king can move and jump backward or forward. A win is scored when an opponent's men are all captured or blocked.

Checkers can be interpreted as war turned into a game on a board. Believe it or not, this "war" game was played by the Egyptians more than three thousand years ago.

 Even the pharaohs were known to enjoy checkers. Not only was it a fun pastime, it was a good way to learn about battle strategy and tactics.

When pharaohs died, they were buried with their favorite belongings—and these items often included their best checkers sets. The belief was that they would be able to play checkers in the afterlife. The British Museum in London has several ancient checkerboards. The boards are similar to those we use today; however, the ancient boards contain fewer squares (usually fifty-two), and the squares are not colored. Instead of alternating dark and light squares, a colorless gridwork was used.

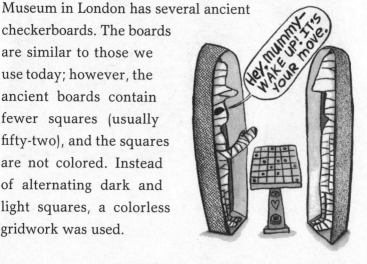

Hey, mummy— WAKE UP! IT'S your move.

The roots of checkers are intertwined with those of chess, a companion game. It is not known for sure which came first. But because checkers is simpler in form, it is generally believed to be the earlier of the two.

Homer, the famous Greek author, mentions checkers in his works. In the *Odyssey,* most likely composed in the eighth century B.C., Homer describes the most famous checkers games of all time. While Ulysses is off to war, his wife is under siege by suitors, men who try to persuade her that Ulysses is dead and that she should marry one of them. To pass the time, the suitors play checkers.

In 1547, Antonio Torquemada of Valencia, Spain, wrote the first book on the tactics and strategy of checkers. Since then, more than two thousand books have been published on what today is considered the world's oldest intellectual game. It is also one of the rarest of games in that, like Twister, it has equal appeal for adults and children.

- The first international checkers tournament took place in 1905. An English team traveled to the United States and won the tournament. In a 1927 rematch, an American team was sent to England and triumphed 96–20.
- One variation of the game is called "losing checkers." The first player to lose all his pieces wins the game.
- Another form of the game, called "international checkers," uses twenty checkers per player and a one-hundred-square board. In this version, men may jump backward as well as forward, and kings may move and jump any distance.
- In England, checkers is called draughts (pronounced *drafts*).

MAGIC ROCKS

The year: 1944. The place: a small store in Southern California. Brothers Jim and Arthur Ingoldsby were putting on an in-store demonstration, trying to interest customers in a new product—a vitamin pill for plants.

The brothers were getting frustrated because no one was paying any attention to them. Instead, most of the

people in the store were gathered around another demonstration. Wondering what all the fuss was about, the two sneaked over and joined the crowd. The demonstrator was holding up a fishbowl in which crystals had been grown to make a "Magic Underwater Garden."

Intrigued, Jim and Art bought a few packets of the strange crystals. At home, they tried them out and found that the crystals worked as advertised: as they absorbed water, they enlarged into all sorts of interesting miniature pinnacles and mountains. But the disappointing thing about them was that the colors were so faint the rocks were almost completely white.

The brothers decided to improve the crystals. First, they studied the crystals under a microscope in order to determine their chemical composition. Next came the hard part—finding a way to make the crystals grow into brightly colored rocks. The rocks would also have to hold their color—and not fade to white. After experimenting with all sorts of dyes and substances, they finally succeeded.

Soon, the brothers were able to produce the rocks in eight brilliant colors. By 1945, they had named their new product Magic Isle Undersea Garden. Jim and Art packaged it by hand and sold it by demonstrating in stores. Because it went over well with customers, store owners were happy to stock the product on their shelves—even though they were dissatisfied with the name. Magic Isle Undersea Garden described the product well enough; it even sounded nice, but it was too long and hard to remember.

The brothers kept coming up with new names under which they sold their product. Incredibly, it took them only a few weeks to figure out the formula, but it took them thirteen *years* to come up with its present name! Not until 1958 did it become Magic Rocks.

By 1960, they had turned over the packaging, marketing, and distribution of Magic Rocks to a Chicago-based toy company. However, the brothers refused to turn over the formula.

Executives at the toy company were worried about this arrangement. What if something should happen to the Ingoldsbys? No one—not even the people at the company—knew the formula for coloring the rocks. If the brothers should die, the formula would die with them.

The company executives had a good point, Jim and Art decided. Finally, a compromise was reached—and the formula was locked in a safe.

Will the secret be revealed? We'll have to wait and see.

The ingredients of Magic Rocks are magnesium sulfate (Epsom salt) and sodium silicate. If you mix these chemicals together, Magic Rocks will grow, but only white ones.

- Magic Rocks grow an average of two to four inches in height. But they won't grow any higher. Even if you combined the contents of two packages, the rocks would only increase in width, not height.
- During the 1960s, decorators used Magic Rocks to create offbeat furnishings such as lamps, coat racks, and table legs.
- Despite what many would think, Sea Monkeys are not an offshoot of Magic Rocks. Actually, Sea Monkeys are a type of shrimp that are able to seal themselves in their eggs until surrounding conditions are right for them to be born.

SUPER BALL

Super Balls have been bouncing around since 1965. Sales took off wildly from the start; they skyrocketed— *millions* of Super Balls were sold in their first few months on the market.

It all started in 1964 when a scientist at a rubber company invented a secret rubbery compound he called Zectron. A fantastic discovery, Zectron had six times the bounce of ordinary rubber. But, unbelievable as it may seem, the company's director saw no use for Zectron and gave the rights to the scientist. The scientist then took Zectron to the Wham-O company, where they immediately realized what a great toy it would make.

Soon, Super Balls were rapidly rolling off the assembly line. That's the end of the story of Super Ball's beginnings, but it's just the start of another super-story.

On January 15, 1967, the Green Bay Packers beat the Kansas City Chiefs 35–10 in the AFL-NFL World Championship Game. The next year the Packers were again world champs, defeating the Oakland Raiders 33–14.

The dust was still settling from this second game when the owners of the pro football teams got together for a meeting. Among other things, they talked about giving the World Championship Game a new, snappier name. At first, nothing came to mind. But then Lamar Hunt, one of the owners, started thinking about something that had happened a few days earlier. Mr. Hunt had been home, idly watching his daughter Sharon play with a high-bouncing Super Ball.

The name clicked in Hunt's head. *Ball* morphed into *bowl*. And just like that, the AFL-NFL Championship Game became the Super Bowl. Strange

but true: America's biggest one-day sports event was inspired by a children's toy.

○ During the 1960s, more than 20 million Super Balls were sold.

In the late 1960s, Wham-O produced a giant Super Ball as a promotional item. The huge ball accidentally fell out of a twenty-third-floor hotel window in Australia. It bounced back up fifteen floors, then plummeted down again . . . and crashed into a parked convertible car. The car was destroyed, but the ball survived the accident in perfect condition.

For nighttime play, there are now Glowing Super Balls. Each has ribbons of glowing patterns inside.

For pooches, inventor James Borell has created the Dog-Gone Super Ball. The specially designed ball (it has a tail) takes playing catch with your dog to new heights.

TOY TRAINS

The first real train was called a wagonway. Built in 1550 in France, the contraption was used to haul coal from mines. It ran on wooden tracks and was propelled by a series of large iron pins. The pins, in a narrow groove between the tracks, moved the wagonway along in conveyor-belt fashion.

Toy trains soon followed. Made of wood or tin, the earliest trains were pull toys known as floor-runners. A long cord was attached to the train, making it easy for children to pull along.

I fill mine with bowling pins.

Windup toys were invented in Germany during the Middle Ages. By the sixteenth century, a toy train powered by a top appeared. To operate the toy, a top was stuck into a gear beside the track. The top was then wound up and made to start spinning. As it spun, the gear turned and the train slowly circled the small track.

Toy trains powered by windup mechanisms date back to the 1700s. The first steam-powered toy trains were invented in 1838, though their manufacture did not become widespread until the 1880s. These early steam engine toys became fairly common in Europe, but not in the United States.

Around the turn of the twentieth century, an American teenager, Joshua Lionel Cohen, invented a miniature railroad car. Unlike earlier toy trains, Joshua's was powered by electricity. It worked well, but it looked more like an open cigar box on wheels than a boxcar.

Initially, Josh used his electric train just to amuse himself. After loading the car with various items, mostly toys, he'd watch his train go for a journey on the tracks that circled his bedroom. At the age of twenty-one, Josh was still fascinated with his toy train, and continued improving it. One day in 1901, the thought occurred to him that maybe he could sell his invention.

With his electric train under his arm, he approached Robert Ingersoll, the owner of several toy shops in New York. Josh pitched the train as an "animated advertisement." Placed in the display window of one of Mr. Ingersoll's shops, it would carry his toys around its circular track.

Mr. Ingersoll agreed to give the young man's idea a try. He paid $4 for the gadget, and Josh set the train up in a display window.

Early the next morning, Josh returned to the toy store to see how his advertising gimmick was doing. When he looked in the display window, he was disappointed to discover that his train was no longer there. Upset, he rushed inside and asked Mr. Ingersoll what had happened to his train.

Mr. Ingersoll smiled warmly, and told Josh to relax. Josh's train had been a big hit, but not quite in the way they had expected. What had happened, Mr. Ingersoll explained, was that the train display had immediately caught the attention of a passerby. But instead of buying any of the other toys, the man had bought the train!

Josh stood there speechless.

When Mr. Ingersoll asked if he could make more trains, Josh said enthusiastically that he could—and that he would start right away. The two shook hands. Josh was in business.

Josh made another train as fast as he could, and it was purchased within an hour after going up for sale. Robert Ingersoll ordered more and more. Soon, other stores in the area were buying Josh's electric trains.

In 1906, Josh Cohen patented his invention, improved it greatly, and then started his own company. In naming the company, he used his middle name—Lionel. Though other companies would eventually follow, Lionel was truly the first name in toy trains—and has become by far the best known.

From the start, Lionel trains were marketed for boys and their fathers. Early advertisements included girls only in the background, admiring what their fathers and brothers were doing.

Half a century passed before the Lionel company realized its mistake and changed its marketing strategy. In 1957 the company introduced what is now known as "The Girl's Train." The train set came in pastel colors—including a pink locomotive, yellow boxcars, and a blue caboose. But this train set did not go over well. What the directors of the company failed to realize was that girls wanted the real thing. In fact, girls who received such trains as gifts almost always ended up painting their colorful toy trains black!

Today the Ingersoll Company has a special Visitors Center in Chesterfield, Michigan, that contains a huge wall-to-wall layout of miles of track crisscrossing a make-believe scale-model world. Thirteen transformers power eight trains that simultaneously race across fields, around hills, over bridges, and through miniature cities and towns. Two more trains circle the inside of the building on tracks suspended from the ceiling.

It all started with a teenager devising an electric box that ran on homemade tracks. An interesting sales gimmick—that's all that Joshua Cohen had been trying to make. But instead he created one of the most loved toys of all time.

The all-time bestselling and favorite car of Lionel trains is the milk car. When the train stops, a little man comes out and delivers milk cans, one by one, onto a platform.

○ The few female toy train sets in pastel colors are valuable curiosities today, and collectors will pay top dollar for them.

○ Each year, Lionel produces more than a million engines, cabooses, and other railroad cars. If hitched together, they would make a train about fifty miles long.

○ At the Cleveland Medical Lab, the ore-dumping car of an electric toy train is used to transport radon, a radioactive material. Using remote controls, the operator brings the train from the storage room, stops it at the right spot, then tips the ore car to drop the radon capsules down a chute.

○ A California coffee shop features a toy train, the tracks for which are laid out on the dining counter. The train delivers hamburgers, sodas, and shakes to customers. After customers remove their order, the train backs up and returns to the kitchen.

PLAY-DOH

Originally, Play-Doh only came in white. There's a good reason for this. You see, Play-Doh didn't start out as a toy. It started out as a product for cleaning wallpaper.

In the early 1950s, young Joe McVicker was working for his dad's company, Kutol Chemicals, in Cincinnati, Ohio. There they manufactured soaps and all sorts of cleaning products for the home. When Joe concocted a white, puttylike substance, he wasn't quite sure if it was good for anything at all. But then he tried it out on the smudges on the wallpaper in his dad's office. Presto! It did a super job of taking off grimy fingerprints and other dirty spots.

Joe talked his dad into selling his Magic Wallpaper Cleaner, but sales were slow. The product worked, but people just weren't interested.

Makes nice bookends, too.

One day, Joe was talking on the phone to his sister-in-law, who worked as a nursery school teacher in New Jersey. As they talked, she mentioned that the modeling clay used in her class was too firm for the children's small hands and fingers. And if she added water to make it softer, it made a big mess.

After hanging up, Joe had an idea. He wondered if his wallpaper cleaner might be the answer to his sister-in-law's problem. Joe quickly mailed her several packages. The substance was nontoxic, easy to work with, and stayed soft indefinitely if kept in sealed containers. Teachers and kids alike gave it top grades.

Joe McVicker realized he was on to something. Calling his product Magic Clay, he demonstrated it to teachers

in the Cincinnati area. They were sold on it, and so was the Cincinnati Board of Education: they decided to buy the product for all the kindergartens and elementary schools in the city. Next, Joe took Magic Clay to a large education convention. Owners of toy stores knew a good thing when they saw it and ordered tons of Magic Clay. Before long, it was popping up all over the country.

By 1956, the former wallpaper cleaner had been renamed Play-Doh and Kutol Chemicals had become Rainbow Crafts. In 1957, Dr. Tien Liu, a company chemist, figured out how to whip up batches of Play-

Doh in red, blue, and yellow. Eventually they also made green, purple, pink, orange, and many other colors. And, don't forget, there's still plain white—in case you want to clean your wallpaper!

- Modern Play-Doh has a softer, more pliable consistency than the original.
- The ingredient that gives Play-Doh its distinctive aroma is vanilla.
- Artists, architects, and engineers have been known to use Play-Doh when developing new ideas.
- A model of Monticello, Thomas Jefferson's home in Virginia, has been constructed using more than 2,500 handmade Play-Doh bricks.

TABLE TENNIS

Like several other sports—such as bowling and billiards—table tennis was inspired by bad weather. Basically, it's an indoor version of the outdoor game of tennis. Some say it was invented on a cold, rainy day in South Africa. Others say it got its start in the United States. And still others argue that it was first played by British army officers stationed in India. However, most experts agree that it came into being in England around 1890.

The original table tennis equipment was all home-made. The ball was tightly wound string. Books put down the middle of a table served as the first net. The paddles were cut from thick pieces of cardboard.

As the game gained popularity, the equipment improved. The books were the first thing to go. An old badminton net was cut down to size and hung across a dining room table. In another version, the net was strung between the backs of chairs and the game played on the floor.

Balls of cork or rubber soon replaced those of string. Some of the balls were covered with cloth or knitted webbing. Originally, the purpose of this outer cover was to slow the ball down and to cushion the impact on household furnishings. But it was soon discovered that it also made the game more fun by causing the ball to spin in all sorts of fantastic ways.

The balls we use for table tennis today were invented in the United States as toys for toddlers. On a visit to America in 1901, Englishman James Gribb noticed a group of children playing with hollow celluloid balls of various colors. Returning to England with a suitcaseful of the balls, he tried them out at table tennis—and found they were perfectly suited to the game.

The original cardboard paddles fell apart very quickly; a sturdier substance was needed. Wood, you'd think, would have been the obvious choice. It wasn't. Instead, somebody invented a truly bizarre contraption—a paddle with an exceedingly long handle and a hollow striking surface. Covered with hard leather, it looked—and sounded—like a little drum.

Finally, the obvious was hit upon—wooden paddles. They were shaped like the ones we use today and were also about the same size and weight. But there was a problem: the surface was too slick to give players much control over the ball.

In 1904, table tennis enthusiast E. C. Goode was in need of a remedy for a headache. Noticing a studded rubber mat on the drugstore counter, the thought came to him that it might make an excellent surface for a table tennis paddle. His headache forgotten, Goode bought the mat. He took it home, cut it down to size, then glued it to a paddle.

The new paddle gave Goode a lot more control over the ball. In fact, it improved Goode's game so much that he challenged the British national champion. Goode beat him fifty games to three!

Manufacturers of sporting goods competed, too—each coming out with their own set of equipment packaged under their particular name for the game. Among the names used were Gossima, Whiff-Whaff, House Tennis, and Flim Flam.

The Parker Brothers company of Massachusetts was also looking for a trade name for their version. One day in 1920, an employee noticed that when the ball hit the table, it sounded like *pong;* and when it hit the paddle, the sound was *ping.* And just like that, a great new name

for the game was born: Pong-Ping! Of course, a little improvement was needed here, in this case a switch in the word order. And it's been Ping-Pong ever since.

- At the 1956 World Table Tennis Championships, Richard Bergmann of England held up a match for an hour because the ball in use was "too soft and not really round." He examined 192 balls before he found one to his liking.
- The longest-ever Ping-Pong rally in a championship match occurred in 1936. The rally lasted for one hour and fifty-eight minutes.
- The youngest international champion in table tennis (and in *any* sport, for that matter) was eight-year-old Joy Foster of Jamaica.
- Twenty-one has been the winning score in Ping-Pong since the earliest days of the game.
- The highest recorded speed for a Ping-Pong ball is 105.6 miles per hour.

FROM PINBALL TO VIDEO

The first-ever arcade game was called Bagatelle. Extremely popular during the nineteenth century, it was played on a cloth-covered oblong board. The object of the game was for players, using a cue stick, to shoot balls into nine numbered scoring cups. Basically, it was sort of an oddball offshoot of billiards.

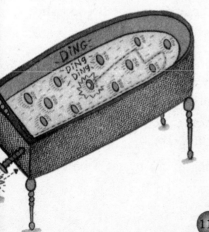

In 1871, a man named Montague Redgrave greatly modified Bagatelle. Instead of a cue stick, a spring plunger was used to knock the ball into motion. He also added pins, which altered the ball's direction, and bells, which sounded when a score was made. All in all, Redgrave's changes mark the true beginning of pinball.

Amusement arcades first began to appear in the United States in the latter half of the nineteenth century. Though games of skill or chance were to be found in arcades, they usually took a backseat to fortune-telling machines, strength-testing devices, and mechanical peep shows. Not until the 1920s did games—especially pinball games—become a common feature in American arcades.

Whoopee, Billiard Skill, Little Whirl-Wind were all pinball games of the Roaring Twenties. But the most successful was Baffle Ball, invented in 1927 by David Gottlieb. Onto a horizontal playing field, the player shot seven steel balls one at a time at four circular scoring areas. A ball that landed in a cup called the Baffle Point doubled the score of the entire table, provided it was not knocked off by subsequent balls. More than anything else, it was this point-doubling feature that made Baffle Ball so popular. Within a year of its invention, four hundred of the machines were being produced every day.

Banging. Knocking. Jiggling. Players of the early machines did all these things to try to get a ball into a desired hole. They also smacked the bottom of the machine—that was the most popular technique of all. By doing this, a player could jar a ball out of one scoring hole into another. To put an end to this practice, a manufacturer named Harry Williams came up with a crude but effective idea. Nails, with their points outward, were hammered into the bottom of the machine. To say the least, anybody trying to slap the table underneath got a painful surprise.

In 1931, Williams devised a gentler anti-cheating device. The device, called a "stool pigeon," consisted of a steel ball set atop a pedestal. If the machine was knocked around too much, the ball fell, immediately stopping play.

Williams eventually came to be known as "the father of modern pinball." The reason: he turned pinball into an electric game. First he added ordinary doorbells. Then came electric buzzers, flashing lights, and an automatic scoreboard. And then Williams added another feature—one that made playing pinball illegal!

The new addition was an automatic pay-out device. For winning a number of games in a row, the player received a small handful of coins. Church groups and politicians complained that pinball had become a gambling game. Newspapers carried stories that linked pinball salesmen with organized crime. Because of these charges many citizens picketed arcades. In 1939, Atlanta, Georgia, became the first city to pass a law against pinball playing.

The punishment was a $20 fine and a month in jail. In 1941, Fiorello La Guardia, up for reelection as mayor of New York City, even went so far as to destroy pinball machines with a sledgehammer.

Many other American cities soon jumped on the anti-pinball bandwagon. Most banned not only the pay-out version of the game, but pinball machines of any kind.

Interestingly, it was another addition to pinball machines that saved the game. In 1947, the Gottlieb company made a machine with flippers— the small arms near the bottom of the board controlled by buttons on the sides of the machine. By using the flippers, a player could keep a ball in play indefinitely.

Hoping to get their machines back into arcades, pinball manufacturers took their case to federal court. With the pay-out device gone, they argued, pinball was no longer a gambling game, and adding flippers had changed it into a game of skill.

The court agreed, and pinball was back.

Soon, old games were being dusted off and set up for play. At the same time, all sorts of new games were invented. In the early 1960s, a group of computer engineers in the United States began toying with the concept of combining pinball and video. In 1962, they created Spacewar, the first-ever computerized video game. Because Spacewar's inventors were only interested in amusing themselves and not in marketing the product, the item never appeared in stores.

In 1972, a man named Nolan Bushnell started the Atari company to make and sell video games similar in design to Spacewar. The first product that the company came out with was called Pong, a tennislike game. By today's standards, Pong was a very primitive and uninteresting version of real-life tennis. Still, it was a start—and the beginning of the most exciting new product line in the recent history of the toy industry.

Soon, all sorts of new games were being invented, most of them intended for home use rather than arcades. By 1975, three short years after the invention of Pong, the Atari company alone was

producing more than a hundred games. By 1976, manufacturers had come out with games that could be played by two people at once, games with multilevel playing fields, and most important, games with a machine that had true video game features. Called the Spirit of '76, this game used electronic blips and flashes instead of steel balls.

From billiards to pinball to video—at first glance, the three games seem so different from each other, but they're not. In numerous and often surprising ways, their histories are intertwined.

- Despite the competition from video games, pinball machines are as popular today as ever. Arcade owners consider them an indispensable attraction.

- A new pinball machine costs over $1,000. That's not a lot of money when you consider that the profit from one machine is $10,000 to $15,000 a year.

- More than 60 percent of all pinball machines manufactured in the United States are exported to other countries.

- The Kampf Flipper, a pinball machine invented in Germany, is played by four players simultaneously.

- By 1984, Atari was facing stiff competition from Nintendo, a Japanese company.

- Sophisticated video games depend on microprocessors. First introduced in 1976, a microprocessor is a tiny computer chip that contains and processes all of the needed information to play the game.

- By 2014, worldwide sales for video games were $1.6 trillion.

TRIVIAL PURSUIT

Scott Abbott and Chris Haney had a lot in common.
Both were in their twenties. Both worked for the same
newspaper—Scott as a sportswriter and
Chris as a photo editor. And both loved
to play Scrabble.

On December 15, 1975, the two got
together with a new game of Scrabble.
As a matter of fact, it was their eighth new Scrabble
game, due to the tendency of game pieces to get lost.
While they played, Chris and Scott started to talk about
inventing a game all their own.

But how do you get into the game business?
they wondered. Where would they get the
money to start up such an enterprise?
And, of course, the biggest question of all:
what type of game would they create?

Obviously, all these questions had their effect. The game, Chris and Scott concluded, should center around questions—all sorts of fun, interesting, entertaining questions. At first they called their game Trivia Pursuit. Chris's wife suggested Trivial Pursuit. It was a small change, but a good one, they agreed—it just sounded better.

The two formed a company, and eventually persuaded Chris's brother John Haney and his friend Ed Werner to join them. Then they started borrowing cash from everybody they knew. In fact, of the original thirty-four investors, one was a copyboy from their newspaper who borrowed the money from his mom.

After they had gathered $40,000, they rented office space for manufacturing, packaging, and selling Trivial Pursuit. But they couldn't pay their helpers much. In fact, instead of a salary, they had to resort to paying many on their staff with shares in the fledgling company.

The first 1,100 sets cost $75 each to manufacture. They sold these to retailers for $15 a game. Obviously, the two young entrepreneurs were having trouble with the trick of turning a profit—losing $60 per sale. By early 1982, Chris and Scott were deeply in debt.

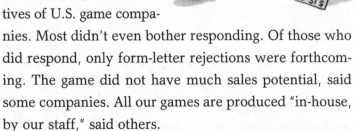

They then began contacting representatives of U.S. game companies. Most didn't even bother responding. Of those who did respond, only form-letter rejections were forthcoming. The game did not have much sales potential, said some companies. All our games are produced "in-house, by our staff," said others.

Chris and Scott were about to quit. Then it happened. The United States game company Selchow and Righter expressed interest in the game. Letters were exchanged, soon followed by phone calls. A meeting was held; an offer was made and accepted. Trivial Pursuit was on its way!

Selchow and Righter hired a public relations consultant who immediately launched a powerful advertising campaign. Eighteen hundred of the top buyers at the 1983 New York Toy Fair were sent brochures and copies of the game. And then, for good measure, brochures and game sets were mailed to numerous actors, actresses, and other people in the entertainment industry.

Word of mouth took over. By late 1983, three and a half million games had been sold. In the following year, more than twenty million were bought. Retail sales have now exceeded $1 billion, and show no sign of slowing down.

Today, people play Trivial Pursuit in nineteen different languages in more than thirty different countries.

The questions are modified to suit the interests, customs, and histories of each particular country. And there are many versions, such as the Baby Boomer Edition, All-Star Sports Edition, Kids Edition, Trivial Pursuit–Star Wars, and even an electronic variation of the game. Not to be forgotten is the original version: the Master Game–Genus Edition.

On the box of the original game there is a quote from *The Rape of the Lock*, a poem written in the eighteenth century by Englishman Alexander Pope. Quite fittingly, it reads: "What mighty contests rise from trivial things."

Toy Trivia Questions

1. What game did crossword puzzle lover Alfred Butts invent in 1931?

2. The Arabic phrase *al shah mat* means "the king is dead." In chess, into what game-ending word does this phrase translate?

3. What toy gets its name from a Hawaiian dance?

4. After which United States president are teddy bears named?

5. What toy did Donald Duncan first make from wood, and then begin making from plastic in 1957?

6. The board of what bestselling game contains the names of actual streets and places in Atlantic City, New Jersey?

7. Which United States president played marbles and married Martha Custis?

8. What toy truck company takes its name from a Dakota Sioux Indian word meaning "great"?

Answers

1. Scrabble 2. Checkmate 3. Hula Hoop 4. Teddy Roosevelt 5. Yo-Yo
6. Monopoly 7. George Washington 8. Tonka

KITES

Invented in China, kites have been around for at least three thousand years. Since their beginning, they've been used primarily as toys. But kites have had other uses, too, and that's the best part of their story.

Like fishing with kites. It sounds hard to believe, but that's one use to which they've long been put in China and other Asian countries. The fisherman stands on shore maneuvering a kite far out over the water. From the tail dangles a hook, line, and sinker. When a fish bites, the kite is jerked upward, then it—and the airborne fish—is reeled in.

Flying kites over houses is a Chinese custom that dates as far back as 1000 B.C.—and is still practiced today, especially at night. Kites are attached by strings to rooftops. The belief is that the kites guard the house and its inhabitants from the evil spirits of darkness.

Similarly, there is even an Asian religion based on kite flying. In one ceremony, participants fly kites as high as possible. The higher the kite goes, it is believed, the closer the person is to heaven. Many of the kites carry pictures for one's ancestors to see and messages for them to read.

In China, dating to 1000 B.C., kites were used by the military as signaling devices, most often to warn of an enemy attack. Different colored kites indicated the number of troops and the direction from which they were coming. At night, for the same purpose, tiny lanterns of different colors were raised on the kites.

Around 500 B.C., the Chinese took this concept to a whole new level. Huge kites were built—kites big and strong enough to support a person! First, the soldier would lie with his legs extended across the kite and grab hold of special handgrips. Then, using a stout cord, several soldiers would tow the kite until it rose high into the air. Once aloft, the man would have a clear view of the enemy on the ground, and, using flag and hand signals, relay information back to his officers. Sometimes the kite was let out far enough so that it was almost right above the enemy. Bows and arrows, catapults, and even cannons were used to try to bring down the kite and its rider!

The earliest known kites in Europe date from the early fourteenth century, when the military began using them as banners. Each unit had its own kite. As they headed into battle, the high-flying kites identified the different units and where they were located on the field.

Near the end of the fourteenth century, Europeans began doing what the Chinese had done hundreds of years earlier. They started using kites as wartime signaling devices. Different sizes, shapes, colors, and designs were employed to send whatever message was needed.

Not until the twentieth century—more than five hundred years later—did the European military employ man-carrying kites. Although the goal was the same—to spy on enemy territory—the technique, utilized by the British in 1904, was much different from the one invented by the Chinese. The British made use of what is known as a box kite, a kite which has paper or fabric at both ends that form squares. First, a long train of box kites was put up in the air. Then another box kite, with a man inside, was run up a line to whatever height was desired. Using a train of several kites was more stable than a single kite, and it enabled the observer to reach greater heights.

Kites were used for military purposes as recently as World War II. Like the Chinese and British, the Germans sent them up as observation platforms. But there was an interesting difference between these and previous man-carrying kites. They were towed along, high up in the air, by German U-boats traveling on the surface.

During World War II, the United States had its own use for kites—not for banners, for sending messages, or for carrying lookouts. The United States Army employed kites to give soldiers antiaircraft training. Large kites with the silhouettes of airplanes painted on them were sent aloft. The soldiers would then fire at the kites to improve their aim.

Americans have put kites to all kinds of other uses as well. For over a hundred years, they were the primary means of getting information about the weather. Fitted out with an array of instruments, they could obtain data like never before. Though planes, weather balloons, and satellites have now taken over this role, it was kites that led the way.

This kite shows us it's a windy day!

People have even used kites in the building of bridges. For example, a kite line was used to start the building of the first suspension bridge at Niagara Falls. Once the line was carried over the river by a kite, a heavier line was attached to it, then pulled across.

Throughout their history, kites have been put to all sorts of fascinating and surprising uses. Today, they are used purely for entertainment. Flying a kite is certainly fun but so is making one. Try it. Come up with your very own design, shape, and color and then let your kite soar. The sky is the limit.

Since the first man-carrying kites were made around 500 B.C., kites were, in a sense, the first aircraft in history.

- Kites were named in the sixteenth century after the kite, a type of bird in the hawk family. Kites have a broad wingspan, a long, tapering tail, and the ability to remain in one place in the air by heading into the wind.

- Centuries ago in Polynesia, kings flew kites over their royal habitat to identify themselves to the gods they worshiped.

- In Hawaii, kites were once used to establish land ownership. A kite would be released and a claim would be made to the area where it fell.

- The first wartime aerial photographs were taken by cameras mounted on kites. United States troops used them in 1898 during the Spanish-American War.

- The highest kite ever flown was one used for gathering weather information. It rose to an incredible elevation of 23,835 feet.

DOLLS

The earliest dolls were for the dead. Found in three-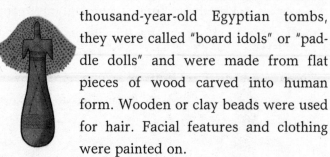thousand-year-old Egyptian tombs, they were called "board idols" or "paddle dolls" and were made from flat pieces of wood carved into human form. Wooden or clay beads were used for hair. Facial features and clothing were painted on.

Board idols were buried with adults as well as children; their purpose was to accompany the deceased on their journey to the spirit world. This custom replaced an earlier and much more grisly one—burying slaves alive with their masters! The belief was that the slaves would continue to serve and protect their owners in the afterlife.

In 700 B.C., Greek and Roman children played

with jointed clay dolls. With iron pins to give them movable arms and legs, the dolls were primitive action figures and could also be used for playing dress-up. By 300 B.C., children had soft dolls made from brightly colored knitted wool or fabric stuffed with dried grass.

When Greek and Roman girls were old enough to marry—usually thirteen or fourteen—they gave their favorite dolls to statues of goddesses. (In Rome it was Venus, the goddess of beauty; in Greece it was Diana, the goddess of purity and hunting.) This was symbolic of the young woman giving up the possessions of childhood for those of adulthood.

Adult Romans kept "ancestor dolls." After a family member died, a likeness of the person was carved from wood and placed on the fireplace mantel with other such dolls. From there, it was believed, they watched over the household, protecting it from harm. At mealtimes, the ancestor dolls were sometimes brought to sit at the table, and small dishes of food were placed before them.

Many Asian countries of the time had their own versions of ancestor and funeral dolls as well as soft, jointed dolls for play. The Japanese also had "friendship dolls." Most often, these were given to people visiting one's home for the first time.

Perhaps the most unusual Asian dolls were those

used by Chinese doctors as late as A.D. 8. Only men could be doctors at that time, and because it was considered improper for them to examine women, a curtain separated the physician and the female patient. On a porcelain figurine, the woman would mark the area of the body that was bothering her, hand it through the curtain, and then discuss her problem with the doctor.

During the Middle Ages (A.D. 400–1500), many dolls were religious in nature. In Europe, they were of the Christ Child or the Virgin Mary. At about the same time in Africa and the West Indies, voodoo dolls were used in religious rites based on sorcery and the casting of spells. The Hopi and other Native Americans created Kachina dolls, personifications of spirits believed to carry people's prayers to the gods.

Another interesting type were "fashion dolls." Beginning in the fourteenth century, women in different parts of Europe sent such dolls to friends to show new clothing styles. Queen Anne of England ordered the earliest set of fashion dolls on record from France in 1391.

Not until the 1600s in Germany were "baby dolls" manufactured on a large scale. Most were wooden. People usually bought them unclothed and then sewed clothing for them at home.

By the 1800s, Europeans and Americans were making dolls from a wide range of materials. Porcelain, wood, plaster, wax, and papier-mâché (paper pulp) were all used. Ms. Isannah Walker of Rhode Island made hers of stiffened fabric. In the 1840s, she became the first U.S. manufacturer to mass-produce dolls; during this period she invented a machine for pressing layers of glued cloth together and molding them into a lifelike shape.

By the late 1800s, many dolls had glass eyes that could be opened or closed by pulling a string. Some had hair made of wool or animal fur. More costly were those with human hair, which had to be sewn into the head with a hot needle, one strand at a time. Eyelashes were added in the same manner. The overall result was a doll with a jointed, padded body covered with soft, skinlike fabric.

During this time, most dolls were infant "baby dolls," and their primary purpose was to help prepare little girls for motherhood—for feeding, clothing, and otherwise taking care of newborns. The famous French author Victor Hugo even suggested that the first child a woman has is a continuation of her last doll.

By the twentieth century, dolls had been invented that could talk, walk, or even dance to the tune of a music box inside their bodies. More and more were being made of rubber, celluloid, or plastic.

In 1910, American artist Rose O'Neill created the Kewpie doll, using her baby brother as a model. The comical little doll—like its real-life counterpart—always had a tuft of hair at the top of his head. Such dolls were given as prizes at carnivals, fairs, and amusement parks.

During the same era, U.S. companies began offering dolls as advertising premiums. For a given number of box tops or labels, kids could send away for Aunt Jemima (pancake mix and syrup) dolls or Campbell Kid dolls from the Campbell's Soup Company.

From the 1930s on, comic books, movies, and television shows gave rise to "character dolls." Such dolls were made in the likeness of well-known political figures, entertainers, and cartoon characters—such as Donald Duck, Batman, and Zorro.

Barbie—what a doll! Introduced in 1959, Barbie was a hit from the start, and she soon became the top-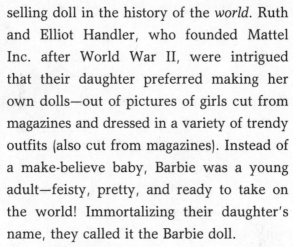selling doll in the history of the *world*. Ruth and Elliot Handler, who founded Mattel Inc. after World War II, were intrigued that their daughter preferred making her own dolls—out of pictures of girls cut from magazines and dressed in a variety of trendy outfits (also cut from magazines). Instead of a make-believe baby, Barbie was a young adult—feisty, pretty, and ready to take on the world! Immortalizing their daughter's name, they called it the Barbie doll.

In 1961, the Handlers came out with a boy doll, Ken, named after their son. Expecting a sales ratio of five to one, they were pleasantly surprised to find they were two to one, one Ken for every two Barbies.

Barbie has been a flight attendant, an astronaut, a singer—she is a new-age girl with unlimited potential.

Rivaling Barbie's phenomenon are American Girl dolls. First created by a Wisconsin woman, the lifelike eighteen-inch dolls depict American girls throughout history—from our earliest days to the present. Kirsten—she's a strong and spirited pioneer girl; Felicity—a spunky girl living in Virginia just before the Revolutionary War; Kaya— an adventurous Native American beauty growing up in 1764; Addy—a courageous girl escaping slavery in 1864; Kit—a clever, quick-witted girl growing up in Cincinnati in 1934. And then there's Josefina, Nellie, Julie, Kanani, and so many more, each doll showing what life was like for preteen girls coming of age during different periods of American history.

First produced by the Pleasant Company in 1986 by educator Pleasant Rowland, the dolls are sold with accompanying books told from the viewpoint of the girls they represent. And, as with Barbie, a wide range of outfits and accessories are also available—historically accurate, of course.

○ The word *doll* comes from the Greek word for "idol," *eidolon.*

○ In America, the earliest dolls are thought to be

those found in Aztec graves, all predating the conquest of Mexico in the sixteenth century.

○ "Mama dolls," invented in 1824 in Germany, were the first talking dolls. Chatty Cathy, introduced by the Mattel Company in 1959, is far more talkative; when her string is pulled, she blurts out such things as "I want a drink of water"; "Let's play house"; or "Please change my dress."

○ Queen Victoria of England (1819–1901) played with dolls until she was fourteen—and became queen at seventeen. As an adult, she collected dolls and sewed clothes for them. On a whim, she would give dolls to friends, visitors, servants—even to people on the streets, usually children.

○ "Penny woodens" were jointed wooden dolls popular in the nineteenth century. Queen Victoria's collection included more than a hundred penny woodens.

○ Cabbage Patch Kid dolls, with a plastic head, yarn hair, and soft, huggable bodies were a huge (but rather short-lived) fad in the 1980s. Production could not keep up with demand, and fist fights broke out in stores between potential buyers. They were the concept of Xavier Roberts, a young artist who envisioned a magic world in which dolls grew in fields like cabbages.

- In Iran in 2002, Barbie was a bestseller despite its $40 price tag—in a country where the average monthly salary was $100. In the same year, Iranian toy makers came out with their own version of the dress-up doll, one with a traditional Muslim wardrobe.
- Barbie's official birthday is March 9, 1959, the date she made her doll-world debut at the International American Toy Fair in New York City, which means Barbie turned 75 in 2014.

HOT WHEELS

Less than ten years after the Mattel Toy Company introduced Ruth Handler's Barbie doll, her husband, Elliot (one of Mattel's founders), created Hot Wheels.

What Elliot Handler had in mind were die-cast metal cars with working wheels covered with styrene, a type of plastic. Set in motion down a ramp, the car would then shoot around a track. He wanted the cars to be miniatures of real makes on the road—Fords, Chryslers, and Pontiacs, for example.

Elliot put together a development team—a group of men and women who would work with him to make the prototype, the original working model.

First, the team decided on the type of car to create in miniature. Because it was a fast sports car with sleek lines, they settled on the Chevy Camaro.

After every detail of the full-size vehicle was photographed and measured, draftsmen drew blueprints at one sixty-fourth the size of the actual car. With the photographs and blueprints spread before him, an artist called a pattern maker carefully carved a wooden replica. To make it easier to work on, the replica was four times larger than the toy would be.

From the wooden model of the Camaro, an epoxy (hard plastic) "pattern" was made. Then, using the pattern as a guide, master toolmakers fashioned steel molds in the shapes of the car's wheels, body, chassis, interior, and engine. Some of the molds were filled with molten metal, others with liquefied plastic, depending on the car part being made. (For example, plastic was used for the interior.)

Finally, the parts were painted, assembled, and tested. The end result was an exact miniature of a real Chevy Camaro. From the hubcaps to the door handles, every detail was the same.

When the production team was ready with the prototype, they put on a demonstration for Elliot Handler. The toy car was everything he'd wanted—and more. With its low-friction styrene wheels, it could

reach an estimated scale speed of 200 miles per hour as it shot down a steep track—powered by gravity and a later-discontinued internal drive mechanism (which was activated by pulling the car backward to rev it up).

Seeing the car in action, Handler was amazed at its quality and speed. Using a '60s expression meaning "an extremely cool and fast car," he exclaimed,

Those are HOT WHEELS!

They're even hotter now. Today's Hot Wheels can be rocket-launched by a slingshot. Pushing a release button sends the car racing on a wild ride around a track with more twists, curves, and loops than a roller coaster!

Mattel also makes Hot Wheels for different age

groups. There are simpler designs for young children; older kids like do-it-yourself track systems—a kit containing track sections, connectors, and a launcher.

Sales are as fast and impressive as the cars. Each year, more Hot Wheels roll off assembly lines than real-life Fords, Chryslers, and Pontiacs combined!

- Before there were Hot Wheels, there were die-cast metal cars. In 1945, Fred Ertl of Iowa became the first person to mass-produce toy farm equipment. Ertl, a German immigrant, first made them for his own children, then decided to go into business when he saw how much his kids loved the toys.
- Though the Hot Wheels prototype was a Chevy Camaro, the most popular car has long been the Corvette. The most valuable? It's the Volkswagen Surfer's Van. One in excellent condition is now worth up to five thousand dollars.
- In the first year of production, 1968, Mattel produced a series of sixteen Hot Wheels. Twenty-four new cars were released the following year. Today, more than 700 car makes have been rendered into Hot Wheels, and others are on the way.
- In 1970, promotional Hot Wheels were made for

the restaurant chain Jack-in-the-Box. In 1985, Hot Wheels were given away as premiums in boxes of Kellogg's cereal.

- Over 2.5 million Hot Wheels are sold every week throughout the world.

- In 1971, motorcycles, trains, and airplanes were added to the Hot Wheels line. The first Hot Wheels helicopter hit the market in 1990.

- Though invented in the United States, Hot Wheels are no longer made in this country. In fact, they haven't been since 1971! All are manufactured overseas.

- Hot Wheels cars are produced at the rate of one per second!

- The one-billionth Hot Wheels car was sold in 1991.

MONOPOLY

Monopoly was patented by Charles Darrow in 1935 and went on to become the bestselling game in the United States, as well as in many other countries.

Hold the applause for Mr. Darrow.

The idea for the game was not original. He "borrowed" it from earlier variations. And then he got lucky.

Homemade buying and selling games, most often played by college students, were first created in the 1890s. None were commercial successes; none were patented. No doubt influenced by these early games, Lizzie Magie, a young woman from Virginia, devised her own version at the beginning of the twentieth century—The Landlord's Game. In 1904, she had it patented. The similarities between her game and the later Monopoly cannot be dismissed: they both had forty spaces—including four railroads, two utilities, and twenty-two pieces of property for sale. Additionally there were spaces for jail, luxury tax, and free parking.

Though similar in layout, the purpose of Magie's game was the opposite of Monopoly's. Magie, a Quaker, created her game as a fun way to teach the evils of monopolies, of one person or company taking almost everything while the rest get almost nothing. Magie clearly explains this in her written introduction to the game, and the rules and board are designed specifically to get her message across. For example, all rent is put into the public treasury, college is free, and players are encouraged to share their winnings with others if they become wealthy.

Thirty years later, Charles Darrow entered the picture. He claimed to be the inventor of Monopoly. But in truth he borrowed heavily from Lizzie Magie's game.

During the Great Depression (1929 to 1939), banks and businesses failed worldwide, leaving millions of people jobless and penniless. In the United States alone, thousands lost their homes; many died from cold and starvation. Great numbers of people wandered the country seeking food, shelter, clothing—and jobs. They traveled on foot and by freight train and lived in camps called "hobo jungles."

Charles Darrow of Germantown, Pennsylvania, had it better than most. Though he had lost his job—heating equipment salesman—he and his wife had managed to hold on to their house. Charles made what he could performing odd jobs. Mostly he repaired things—toasters, washing machines, and other electrical appliances. He also walked dogs.

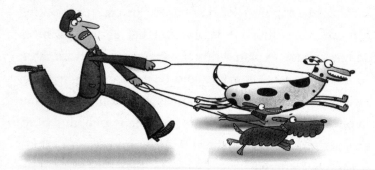

They were barely getting by when Darrow learned his wife was expecting their second child.

Trying to find a way to make more money, and fill his many empty hours, Darrow made toys. He devised an improved score pad for the game of bridge; he made jigsaw puzzles; he even invented a bat-and-ball toy for use at the beach.

When none of these sold, he turned his attention to creating a board game. After all, board games were becoming increasingly popular as a result of the Depression; live theater, movies, and other forms of entertainment were simply too expensive. But board games (then called "parlor games") did not cost a great deal and could be played over and over. In fact, playing board games was the main form of entertainment for the Darrows and their family and friends.

As a kid, Darrow had played The Landlord's Game. Now he decided to make his own version. Relying greatly on Magie's game, he made a prototype of The Game of Monopoly out of a linoleum sheet. On it he painted property squares and gave them the names of real places in Atlantic City, New Jersey, which was his family's favorite vacation spot. Park Place, Ventnor Avenue, and the Boardwalk, for example, were all places that Darrow knew well.

Darrow's family and friends loved playing The Game of Monopoly on the homemade board. It took their minds off their problems, and it gave them a make-believe way to have money and buy property— things the Depression had made impossible in real life.

Soon others wanted their own boards. At $4 apiece, Darrow began making copies for friends— and friends of friends. He painted the game boards using free paint samples. With scraps of discarded wood from a lumberyard, he carved houses and hotels. On thick, stiff paper, he typed up title

cards for the properties. Buyers bought their own dice, tokens, and packages of play money. Though Darrow didn't do any advertising, word spread and he was soon getting orders from all over the country.

Working at top speed, Darrow could produce two complete games a day. A friend helped by printing the title cards and game boards. This increased production to six a day. But Darrow could not supply the ever-rising demand.

In 1934, Darrow worked out an agreement with the same friend to print and package complete sets; Darrow would continue making the wooden houses and hotels. Under this arrangement, up to twenty-five sets could be made a day. For several months the problem was solved, and production kept up with sales. Soon, however, twenty-five games a day was not enough: more requests were coming in from friends and friends of friends for

the handmade game—far more than the partners could possibly produce.

Darrow knew he had to take Monopoly to a profes-sional game manufacturer. He wrote to Parker Brothers and sent them a copy of his game. There, brothers George and

Charles Parker "test-played" Monopoly . . . and gave it a unanimous thumbs-down. One executive wrote, "The concept is dull, the action slow-paced, and the rules hopelessly complex." Another said, "It will never sell. The game contains fifty-two fundamental errors."

Despite this response, Darrow didn't give up. He went from town to town and from store to store, looking for one that would carry his game. No one was interested—until the day he met with the manager of Wanamaker's department store in Chicago. To Darrow's surprise, the manager had one of the original, handmade copies of the game at home and loved playing it. Eagerly he agreed to stock Monopoly on his shelves.

With money earned from earlier sales, and the rest borrowed from family and friends, Darrow and a handful of employees made five thousand sets. At Wanamaker's, Monopoly was a hit from the start. Almost immediately it became the fastest-selling game in the store.

Hearing about the game's success, the executives at Parker Brothers realized that, despite the game's so-called "fifty-two fundamental errors," they were the ones making the mistake. In 1935, they contacted Monopoly's inventor and purchased the rights to make and sell the game, with a large share of the profits going to Charles Darrow.

In 1936, Parker Brothers sold every set they could manufacture and were bombarded with orders for more. As the Christmas season approached, orders were coming in so fast, the games had to be stacked and stored in hallways!

Charles Darrow became a multimillionaire and retired at the age of forty-six to become a "gentleman farmer" in the Pennsylvania countryside. As for George and Charles Parker, Monopoly literally saved them from financial ruin. The truth is, the company had been on the verge of bankruptcy in the early 1930s—right about the time that Darrow happened along with what turned out to be the biggest moneymaking game in history.

- Before Monopoly, Charles Darrow made other board games, none of which he was ever able to sell or manufacture in significant numbers.
- Despite their incredible success, the company's top executives decided that Monopoly was just a fad, one that wouldn't last more than three years. In December 1936, company president George Parker ordered the manufacturing of Monopoly to "cease absolutely. We will stop making Monopoly against

the possibility of a very early slump." But sales of the game had never been higher; to quit making a top-selling game made no sense at all. Before the brakes could be put on production, George Parker changed his mind.

- While Darrow made a fortune on the game, Lizzie Magie, the original patent holder, made next to nothing.

- Monopoly is popular around the world and available in nineteen languages.

POKÉMON

Satoshi Tajiri of Japan invented Pokémon.

As a kid growing up in the 1970s, Tajiri loved to collect bugs. Tromping through the fields and forests near his home on the outskirts of Tokyo, he snagged butterflies with a net, found creepy crawlers under rocks, and collected crabs and crayfish from ponds.

Tajiri also loved monster movies, science-fiction novels, and video games. To make time for his hobbies, he cut class and barely made it through high school.

After he finally graduated, his father decided that Tajiri should go to college or become an electrical utility repairman. Tajiri wasn't the least bit interested in either. Still, to please his dad, he went to a technical school—and spent most of his time in arcades playing video games. He was around so often and was such a likable guy that one of the arcade owners gave him a full-size Space Invaders machine to take home!

At seventeen, he and several friends launched a magazine called *Game Freak*, which at first was handwritten and stapled together. Ken Sugimori happened to pick up a copy and decided he wanted to get involved. The two boys hit it off from the start. Soon they decided that most video games were of poor quality—and that they could make far better ones.

After considerable study, they created an arcade-like game called Quinty, eventually selling it to the company Namco.

The idea for Pokémon popped into Tajiri's head in 1990.

Tajiri had previously worked for Nintendo on The Legend of Zelda and other games. Impressed with his and Ken's work, the Nintendo executives put Pokémon into development.

Six years later the game was ready, and Pokémon—short for Pocket Monster, or *Poketto Monsuta*, as it was called in Japan—hit stores.

The story in the game was a lot like Tajiri's insect-collecting days: a player goes on a strange adventure in a world populated by all kinds of wild creatures—with buggy names like Kingler, Krabby, Grimer, and Squirtle. The player's task is to capture as many Pokémon as possible. Once captured, a Pokémon joins the player's team and helps him or her grab other unsuspecting critters on the way to becoming a Pokémon Master.

The game was an immediate hit in Japan. Its tremendous popularity led to the making of a Japanese Pokémon TV series, a card-trading game, and comics. These spin-offs caused Pokémon's sales to soar. Not only did older kids love them, but younger children could now participate in the craze. And the younger children, of course, were the next generation of Pokémon video-game players.

In 1998, Pokémon invaded the United States—on its way to conquering the world. Over the next two years, a staggering twenty million copies of the video game were sold in the United States alone. Warner Brothers released three big-screen, feature-length Pokémon movies. Books, clothes, stuffed animals, and all sorts of other Pokémon items popped up everywhere.

As for Tajiri, he's a wealthy, fun-loving nut—an eccentric genius who likes to work on his games for twenty-four hours straight, then sleep for twelve. He's living proof of the truth of an old saying: "Find a job doing something you love, and you'll never work a day in your life."

- Pokémon are never killed; they just faint.
- Pokémon video games consist of two interactive Game Boy units, connected via a cord, allowing players to join forces as a team and share information.
- Ken Sugimori illustrated the first 151 Pokémon video games—and most thereafter. He also lent his gifted hand to Pokémon card games and other spin-offs.
- Each Pokémon has a special power. Some can fly; others start fires. Still others just disappear and then turn up someplace else.
- Pokémon all but saved Nintendo. Sales were waning until Tajiri's video game took the world by storm.

SCRABBLE

Alfred M. Butts was a young teen in 1913, the year the crossword puzzle was invented. He loved doing them. A native New Yorker, Alfred would work on crosswords in class, in the streetcar on the way home, or in his favorite hangout, a tree house in his backyard. When Alfred grew up, he kept right at it—only now he did extremely hard crosswords.

The Great Depression of 1929 hit the Butts family hard. Alfred, an architect by trade, was out of work—as were millions of other Americans. With time on his hands, naturally Alfred did countless crosswords. One afternoon in 1933, as he worked away on one, he suddenly had a brainstorm: maybe he could take the basic idea behind the crossword puzzle and turn it into a board game.

Off went Alfred to his workshop behind the house. As he tinkered, the first thing he decided was that there would be no dice in his game. He didn't like them—first, because they were associated with gambling; second, he considered dice games to be mostly luck. Instead, his game would test and develop players' thinking power, especially their word skills.

On a sheet of architect's blue-print paper, he created colored squares, then glued the sheet to a carefully crafted wooden board. Next, he made exactly one hundred little wooden tiles and hand-painted a letter on each. Frequently used letters (especially vowels) appeared most often but had the lowest point value; letters such as J, Q, X, and Z, which are used least often in English and therefore are the hardest to place, had the highest point values. As he worked, Alfred jotted down other rules of the game. And finally he gave it a name: The Game of It.

Alfred was quiet and shy. He was no salesman, and he didn't have interest in selling his game. All he really wanted to do was enjoy The Game of It. Whenever the chance arose with family and friends, he would play the game by the hour.

Years passed. Finally, after repeated attempts, Alfred's wife succeeded in getting him to do two things. First, she persuaded him to change the name—The Game of It became Criss-Cross. Next she talked him into showing his creation to game manufacturers. She was sure they would be smart enough to buy her husband's clever game. They weren't. Instead of interest, the only thing they showed him was the door.

Then 1948 rolled around. Fifteen long years had passed since Alfred invented his game. One of his friends during this time was James Brunot, a social worker. On many occasions, James and his family had played Criss-Cross at Alfred's home. One evening as they played, James had a sudden inspiration.

"We could sell the game—be business partners!" he exclaimed.

"No, I've already tried selling it to some of the big companies," said Alfred. "There's no interest."

"Well then, we could manufacture it ourselves. Start our own company."

Alfred hemmed and hawed. He gave every reason

he could think of to scrap the idea, but James persisted. "How about doing it this way?" he said. "We'll make the games together, but my job will be to sell them. You won't have to do anything on the selling end."

Alfred's eyes brightened. "Well now, *that* might just work."

An agreement was struck, and Alfred and James were in business.

First they changed the name of the game—this time from Criss-Cross to Scrabble. James came up with the name. "Scrabble," he thought, was sort of like the game itself, since the action always started with players scrabbling around after a bunch of tiles.

The first "manufacturing plant" was James's living room. There, the two men and their wives went to work, turning out the games by hand. Soon, because it made a mess of the house, the operation was moved to an abandoned schoolhouse. At that point, Mr. and Mrs. Butts bowed out of the manufacturing end of the business, and the Brunots took over the actual making of the games.

In 1949, their first full year in operation, they assembled 2,251 copies of Scrabble. Though they sold them all (at $3.00 apiece), they were losing money. Making each set was costly and time-consuming, and business was simply not brisk enough to turn a profit.

By early 1952 the Brunots were ready to throw in the towel. Sales had slumped to an average of sixteen games per day. They had hardly enough money to put food on the table let alone pay off their mounting debts.

Please don't throw me in yet!

Then something strange happened. Toward the end of 1952, sales skyrocketed. Overnight, the demand jumped to 107 sets per day. And then it doubled . . . and doubled again! Orders were coming in faster than they could fill them.

The Brunots and the Butts were as baffled as they were pleased. What had caused the game's sudden surge in popularity?

It took a while, but they finally learned the answer: while on vacation, one of the owners of Macy's department stores had played the game and loved it. Returning to New York, he asked his game department to send a few sets up to his office. Learning that none of the Macy's stores carried the game, he immediately gave orders "to stock every store in the country."

Within the year, requests for the game were far beyond what the Brunots could fill. Together with Mr. and Mrs. Butts, they sold the rights to manufacture and sell Scrabble to the Selchow & Righter Company. The two families made a fortune. As for the game, the homemade brainstorm once known as The Game of It is now the second-bestselling board game in the United States, topped only by Monopoly.

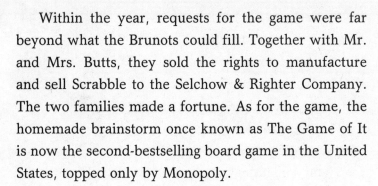

- It took Alfred Butts almost a decade to finalize the letters' point values.
- Scrabble has been translated into more than thirty languages, and a version in Braille has been issued for the blind.
- Alfred Butts was not the only person swept up by the crossword puzzle fad. In the early 1930s, men's shirts and women's dresses, shoes, and handbags were patterned with crossword designs.
- There are now video-game, computerized, and travel versions of Scrabble, not to mention advanced game boards. There are also thousands of Scrabble computer clubs and tournaments around the world.

SKATEBOARDS

Skateboards evolved from homemade scooters, in which the wheels from an old pair of metal skates were nailed to a two-by-four board. In front, the contraption had a wooden box with handles for steering and control.

But some kids wanted no part of the box. They removed it and rode just the board. A new sport had begun.

In the late 1950s, the surfing craze hit the United States, especially California. When the waves were dead, kids went "sidewalk surfing" instead.

Kids began to make changes in the boards. To get a better ride, they used wider, flatter, stronger wooden planks. As for the wheels, they switched from metal to "clay," a hard synthetic composite. They also changed the trucks—the devices that hold the wheels—to make them more maneuverable.

By the 1960s, skateboarding had a huge following, especially among California surfers. Then a man named Larry Stevenson, the publisher of *Surf Guide* magazine, began promoting sidewalk surfing. Skateboarding started taking off. It got another, bigger boost when Larry's company, Makaha, began making and selling the first-ever custom-crafted boards.

In 1963, the first skateboarding contest was held at Pier Avenue Junior School in Hermosa Beach, California. The following year, the Vita-Pakt Juice Company and legendary surfer Hobie Alter joined to create Hobie Skateboards.

Most kids were happy just to travel the streets and sidewalks, but others developed all kinds of tricks and stunts. The really skilled riders took the sport to a whole new level—usually in dry aqueducts or empty swimming pools. Suddenly, kids were skating vertically as well as horizontally!

By early 1965, there were international contests, cross-country skateboarding teams, and even a movie about the sport, *Skaterdater*. More than fifty million skateboards had been sold. But then the industry crashed.

It was all because of the wheels. The clay wheels didn't have enough traction, enough grip on the pavement. Boarders fell, sometimes seriously hurting themselves or pedestrians. Signs went up in malls, parks, and other places forbidding skateboarding.

Sidewalk surfing went underground for a while. Only the most dedicated skateboarders kept the sport alive. During this time, Larry Stevenson perfected the kicktail. Among other things, it enabled skateboarders to simply kick down on the raised back (the tail) to make the board flip up into the skateboarder's hands.

In 1970, surfer and skateboarder Frank Nasworthy had an idea. He visited a plastics factory where roller-skate wheels were made. He found just what he wanted— polyurethane wheels. They fit perfectly on his skateboard, and when he tried them out, he was elated; they gave a wonderfully smooth ride. Why? Because polyurethane

wheels are softer and actually flatten as they touch the sidewalk, giving them far better traction.

In 1973, Frank introduced his new boards, calling them Cadillac Wheels. At first there was some resistance, especially from veteran skateboarders. But it wasn't long before everybody could see how superior polyurethane was to clay. Then, in 1975, the Road Rider Company improved the wheels even further by adding precision ball bearings to reduce friction and increase speed.

In 1976, the first "skatepark" for skateboarders was built in Florida, and soon they were popping up all across the country.

Since its beginning, some people have predicted— even demanded—an end to skateboarding. In the 1980s, skateboarding's popularity crashed again. Skateboard-related injuries caused cities around the country to again ban skateboarding in public places.

In 1984, launch ramps became popular. So, too, did special shoes and clothing for "boarders," including pads and helmets for safety.

Soon, downhill racing on skateboards added a whole new dimension to the sport.

The equipment—and level of skill—continued to improve. By the 1990s, the sport was back, more popular than ever. According to recent statistics, skateboarding is the sixth-largest participant sport in the United States. Today there are nearly seven million skateboarders in the country.

The most famous is Tony Hawk. No one did more to popularize and revolutionize the sport. At the age of nine, on a hand-me-down board, he discovered a passion for sidewalk surfing and was soon performing far beyond his years. By the age of twelve he was winning amateur contests, by fourteen he'd turned pro, and by sixteen he was considered the best skateboarder of all time!

Not content to rest on his laurels, Tony traveled the world over the next few years, skating in contests and putting on demonstrations, exposing tens of thousands to the new sport. Soon he had launched his own skateboard company, Birdhouse Projects, and Pro Skater video games. He also established the Tony Hawk Foundation, through which he has donated more than $4 million to help finance over 500 public skateparks, most of them in impoverished areas of American cities.

- Almost half of all the skateboarders in the United States live in California.
- In Norway, skateboarding is illegal.
- Back in the 1950s, skateboarding tricks were different from those of today. Called "freestyle," it looked almost like ballet dancing on a zooming board.
- Jan and Dean's song "Sidewalk Surfing" further popularized the sport in 1964.
- In 1978, skater Alan "Ollie" Gelfand invented a tricky maneuver that changed boarding forever. By stomping his back foot down on the tail of the kickboard, he flipped the board into the air and jumped on it at the same time. The trick is named the ollie in his honor.

WIFFLE BALL

Back in 1953, in Fairfield, Connecticut, twelve-year-old David Mullany Jr. had a problem: his backyard was too small to play baseball. What should have been a solid hit bounced off a wall and went right back to the baseman for an out. A home run usually meant a lost ball, a broken window, or both.

David and his friends invented their own brand of baseball. For a bat, they used a sawed-off broomstick handle. For a ball, they tried Ping-Pong balls and plastic golf balls.

The good thing about a plastic ball was that it didn't have the weight to break anything or go too far. The problem was that it was too small and light to pitch properly. And a pitcher was what David wanted to be.

His dad, David Mullany Sr., a former semipro player, came to the rescue. A friend working at a nearby perfume factory gave Mr. Mullany a box of plastic balls used as padding to ship bottles of Coty perfume. They were just about perfect: hollow, round, and only slightly smaller than a baseball. David and his dad tried them out as soon as they could.

Mmm, it smells just like a field of daffodils.

The perfume-packing ball had two drawbacks. First, it carried a little too far. Second, it was impossible to throw a curveball with it. And if David ever wanted to become a pitcher, being able to throw a curve was extremely important.

His dad took the balls into the garage and, one by one, cut a different pattern of openings in each.

David and his dad tried out the bunch. The one that worked best, they decided, had eight evenly spaced oblong openings in half the ball; the other half had a solid surface. The ball didn't go too far when whacked. And just as important, a pitcher could throw a curve, a slider—even a knuckleball.

David and his friends loved the new ball. They gave it a name: Wiffle Ball. At the time, "whiff" was a popular term for striking out a batter. The Wiffle Ball solved David Junior's problem.

It also solved his dad's. At the time, David Mullany Sr. was the president of a car wax company, and business was poor. Still, he took the time to help his son, and he ended up inventing a clever new toy. In 1953, he filed for a patent (#2,776,139) on the Wiffle Ball, and with borrowed money he switched his operation from making car wax to manufacturing Wiffle Balls. The new product was a hit from the start!

- Unique in the toy industry, the Wiffle Ball corporation does no advertising.
- The bats and balls are still made in the same small Connecticut factory.
- The original Wiffle Ball bat was wood. For safety reasons, it was changed to plastic in 1959.
- Since the mid-1970s, Wiffle Ball tournaments have been played across the United States and Canada.
- The first Wiffle Ball championship game was played in 1980, and it has continued to be played every year since. The nonprofit event features a miniature field, with six-foot-high home run fences.
- Today there are multiple variations on the first ball. Most have perforations on all sides, usually round or oblong. Some are as large as softballs, others the size of golf balls.

NOVELTY GAGS

Putting a Whoopee Cushion under someone who is about to sit down is an immature thing to do—but it's also great fun. Fake fangs—they're good for a laugh, too. Of course, you have to be careful—such nonsense sometimes shocks people, or maybe even spooks them for a moment. If this happens, naturally there's only one thing you can do: say "I'm sorry" in your most sincere manner and offer your hand . . . and zap 'em with a Joy Buzzer!

Novelty gags. There are hundreds of them. And no joke—a majority of them were invented by the same person: Sam Adams.

As a child, Sam always had a smile on his face and a joke up his sleeve. By the age of thirteen he was a pool shark. After graduating from high school, he bounced around from job to job, in 1908 landing in a New Jersey chemical factory. Soon after starting work, Sam noticed that one powdery chemical always caused everybody to sneeze. No one—including the owner of the company—wanted the substance around. So, when young Sam Adams offered to buy the company's entire stock, the owner was more than happy to oblige.

Cachoo!

Just like that, Sam became the inventor of Cachoo, the world's first-ever sneezing powder. Working alone, he put the powder into little packets and then began selling them to stores. To his delight, just a few weeks after starting his little sneezing enterprise, a Philadelphia company ordered almost *seventy thousand* Cachoos.

Sam's next offering to the gag world was itching powder, soon followed by stink bombs and squirting flowers. The "dribble glass" was his invention, too.

Then came wedding bells. Marriage caused Sam to settle down . . . sort of.

His wife, he noticed, had a habit of always checking up on him when he ate. The minute he put a container of food away—a can of peanuts, a jar of jelly, a bottle of ketchup—she would ask him if he had put the lid back on tightly. Though Sam would assure her he had, she would never trust him and would always double-check to see for herself.

And that's all it took. After he had put a can of peanuts away one afternoon, his wife (as expected) asked the usual question, then (as expected) opened the lid to make sure . . . when a toy snake (quite unexpected) popped up in her face.

She screamed.

He laughed.

And within the week Sam had added the Snake-in-a-Can gag to his peculiar novelty line.

More nutty novelties followed. Over the next sixty years, Sam Adams came up with close to seven hundred! Most were entirely original, but some were based on the ideas of others. For instance, the Joy Buzzer (gizmos for tickling people's palms) had been around for quite a while. Adams simply made a better buzzer— smaller (so it was easier to hide in your hand) and with much more zing to it. As for the Whoopee Cushion, it was invented by a man working for a company in Canada, the owner of which sent samples to Sam to try to interest him in making the item. Sam sat on the idea too long, and the owner of the Canadian company decided to produce the cushions on his own. Later, Sam came out with his own melodious model—the Razzberry Cushion.

Sam Adams has passed on, but he still makes us laugh. Fake fangs. Black drool gum. And, of course, plastic ice cubes with fake flies in them. Sam Adams's name (written in disappearing ink) will never be forgotten!

- Former President George H. W. Bush was a Joy Buzzer lover and sometimes used them on high-powered politicians to get meetings off to a fun, relaxed start.
- The oldest practical joke on record is Cleopatra's bet that she could drink a million dollars' worth of wine. Of course, no one believed there was any way the Egyptian queen could do it—until she dropped a pearl into the wine, drank it, and won the bet.
- Adams's itching powder was extracted from a weed in India. The substance is so potent and toxic it is now banned.
- In the 1980s, there was a shortage of Whoopee and Razzberry Cushions because the type of rubber used to make them was needed to produce rubber gloves.

TOYS!

MR. POTATO HEAD

BONUS MATERIALS

SCRABBLE

PLAYING CARDS

GOFISH

DON WULFFSON

What did you want to be when you grew up?
A veterinarian.

When did you realize you wanted to be a writer?
When I was seventeen.

What's your favorite childhood memory?
Going to football games with my dad.

As a young person, who did you look up to most?
My dad.

What was your favorite thing about school?
Physical education.

What were your hobbies as a kid?
Sports and hiking.

Did you play sports as a kid?
As often as possible.

What was your first job?
My first job was as a research assistant to a professor, copyediting and proofreading his books. When he found he couldn't finish a book, he asked me to write the ending, giving me my first opportunity to write on a professional level.

What book is on your nightstand now?
The Existential Imagination.

How did you celebrate publishing your first book?
By writing another one.

Where do you write your books?
In my home office.

What sparked your interest in toys?
I'm interested in everything.

What was your favorite toy when you were a child?
A scooter my dad built.

What toy are you most nostalgic about?
The scooter.

What was the research process like for this book?
Very interesting and exhaustive.

If you could have an original of any toy throughout history, which toy would you choose?
The first roller skates, "Wheeled Feet."

What makes you laugh out loud?
My friend Paul.

What do you do on a rainy day?
I love to write on rainy days. I also go out just to feel the rain on my face.

What's your idea of fun?
Watching UCLA football.

What is your favorite word?
Dog.

If you could live in any historical period, what would it be?
All of them, past and future.

Who is your favorite historical figure?
Nelson Mandela.

What was your favorite book when you were a kid?
Beautiful Joe: A Dog's Own Story by Marshall Saunders.

If you were a superhero, what would your superpower be?
My power would be to change everything that's wrong with the world.

What do you consider to be your greatest accomplishment?
Being able to take care of my family while writing my books.

What advice do you wish someone had given you when you were younger?
Never give up.

GO FISH

QUESTIONS FOR THE ILLUSTRATOR

LAURIE KELLER

What did you want to be when you grew up?
I remember wanting to be a TV weather person. I was fascinated with weather and liked watching David Compton report the weather on the local Channel 13 news!

When did you realize you wanted to be an illustrator?
Not until I was out of high school. I always loved art and took every art class available all through school, but I didn't realize I could do it as a job until I went with a friend to a student art exhibit at Kendall College of Art and Design. I enrolled there the following fall and got my degree in illustration. I worked for seven years as a greeting card artist for Hallmark before getting into children's books.

What's your most embarrassing childhood memory?
My skirt got stuck in a folding chair in choir practice, and when we were all supposed to stand and sing, I couldn't get up. The choir director was a very *gruff* sort, and when he saw me sitting, he pounded on the piano, stopped everyone from singing, and asked what I was

doing. It was quite humiliating to explain. My face is turning red all over again just thinking about it!

As a young person, who did you look up to most?
My mom.

What was your first job, and what was your "worst" job?
My first job was selling fruit, pushing the cart around at a busy park. It also happened to be my worst job because on the first (and only) day, the manager stuffed ice down my shirt and later told me to call my mom and tell her she didn't have to pick me up because he could give me a ride home. Creepy! Of course I didn't do that. I told her what happened when she picked me up, and she made me quit. Smart mom.

How did you celebrate publishing your first book?
A very nice friend had a publishing party for me! I also celebrate whenever I finish a book by getting Chinese food.

Where do you work on your illustrations?
In my studio. Sometimes in the early sketch stages I sit outside, but most of the art is done inside at my desk.

Where do you find inspiration for your illustrations?
I have a huge collection of books that I like to thumb through, but lately I've been looking on Pinterest. I'm addicted!

What was your favorite toy when you were a child?
I spent many hours playing with Barbie dolls, but I was also obsessed with Lite Brite!

What toy are you most nostalgic about?
My first two-wheeled bike—a purple Schwinn Sting-ray—with a sparkly silver banana seat and high handlebars with streamers!

What was the research process like for this book?
Don provided some photos, but I researched on the Internet for additional photos and background info. I add little jokes and asides, so it's helpful to be aware of fashion, politics, industry, and the "social scene" of a certain time period.

What was the most interesting thing you learned while working on this book?
There were so many things! While illustrating the new chapters, I learned how hundreds of years ago in Asia, women stood behind a curtain and held out dolls to show their doctors where their aches and pains were!

Where do you go for peace and quiet?
A walk by Lake Michigan or in the woods.

Who is your favorite fictional character?
If I had to pick just one, I'd choose Charlie Brown. He's so contemplative and kindhearted, and I love his tenacity despite living in a world that often disappoints him.

If you could travel in time, where would you go and what would you do?

I would zip back to the early 1500s and see if I could be Leonardo's gofer as he painted the Sistine Chapel, for starters. I'm fascinated with that time period anyway, but to see him paint would be amazing.

What do you want readers to remember about your books?

Hopefully, that they had a laugh or two while reading them. One of my favorite things is when people tell me what lines in my books made them laugh. It doesn't get much better than that!

What would you do if you ever stopped illustrating?

If I were ever good enough, I'd love to be a banjo player in a bluegrass band. I've tinkered with the banjo on and off for years—mostly off, until recently. I take lessons again and make time each day to practice. I also get together with some talented musician friends to play music. It makes me 100% happy!

Do you have any strange or funny habits? Did you when you were a kid?

If there are two items left on the shelf at a grocery store and I only need one, I have to buy both because it makes me feel too sad leaving the one by itself. I've been that way ever since I was little. I figured I'd grow out of it, but I think it's actually gotten worse!

As a kid, I didn't like uneven numbers. So when I would run scared up the stairs from the basement, I would step on the third step twice so it would make an even number of steps.

What do you wish you could do better?
Public speaking. I've always been terrified of it and used to avoid it at all costs. It's gotten easier for me over the years, but I'm by no means a natural at it. One thing that has helped is to set really low standards for myself: if I don't cry, faint, or vomit during a presentation, then I've knocked it out of the park! I really admire people who can get up in front of a large group and speak to them as though it's a room full of their best friends.

What would your readers be most surprised to learn about you?
How long it takes me to write my books. Once in a while they come together in a timely manner, but I second-guess myself again and again and again (and again and again), so it really slows down the process. I would love to be able to change that!

Who is your favorite artist?
If I had to pick one, I'd choose Delphine Durand.

What is your favorite medium to work in?
Acrylic paint and collage.

What was your favorite book or comic/graphic novel when you were a kid? What's your current favorite?
Nancy was my most favorite comic book as a kid,

followed by *Richie Rich* and *Little Lulu*. These are proba-
bly hybrid graphic novel/chapter books, but I really
like *Diary of a Wimpy Kid, Captain Underpants,* and *Dear
Dumb Diary.* Janet Tashjian's My Life as . . . books are
very entertaining. The Just Grace books by Charise
Mericle Harper have elements of a graphic novel in them,
and I think they're spectacular.

**What challenges do you face in the artistic pro-
cess, and how do you overcome them?**
I can easily make my illustrations too busy and cluttered.
Sometimes it works okay, but many times I have to go
back in and simplify them.

**If you could travel anywhere in the world, where
would you go and what would you do?**
I've traveled quite a bit around the world, but the place I
most want to go is Alaska. I'd camp and hike and soak up
the great outdoors. Maybe have tea with a grizzly bear?

BIBLIOGRAPHY

Binney, Ruth, ed. *The Origins of Everyday Things.* London: The Reader's Digest Association, 1999.

Boehn, Max Von. *Dolls and Puppets.* Boston: Branford, 1956.

Clark, Kenneth. *Civilization.* New York: Harper & Row, 1969.

Cook, Chris. *Weapons of War.* London: Crescent Books, 1980.

De Bono, Edward. *Eureka!* New York: Holt, Rinehart & Winston, 1974; revised, 1997.

Dodge, Pryor. *The Bicycle.* Paris and New York: Flammarion Books, 1996.

Eden, Maxwell. *Kiteworks.* New York: Sterling Publishing, 1991.

Foley, Dan. *Toys Through the Ages.* New York: Chilton Books, 1962.

Fraser, Antonia. *A History of Toys.* New York: Delacorte Press, 1966.

Garrison, Webb. *How It Started.* Nashville, TN: Abingdon Press, 1972.

Goodman, Nancy. *Discover How Things Work.* Lincolnwood, IL: Publications International, 1996.

Harris, Henry. *Model Soldiers*. London: Octopus Books, 1962.

Hart, Clive. *Kites, an Historical Survey*. New York: Mount Vernon Publishers, 1982.

Hillier, Mary. *Automata and Mechanical Toys*. London: Jupiter Books, 1976.

Hoffman, D. *Kid Stuff*. San Francisco: Chronicle Books, 1996.

Javna, John, and Gordon Javna. *The '60s!* New York: St. Martin's Press, 1988.

Johnson, Peter. *Toy Armies*. New York: Doubleday, 1982.

Kelly, David. "Ant Farm Creator's Lowly Workers Still Pull Their Weight in a High-Tech World." *Los Angeles Times*, August 5, 2002.

Ketchum, William. *Toys and Games: The Smithsonian Illustrated Library of Antiques*. New York: Cooper-Hewitt Museum, 1981.

King, Constance. *The Encyclopedia of Toys*. New York: Crown Publishers, 1978.

Kitahera, Teruhisa. *Yesterday's Toys: Planes, Trains, Boats, and Cars*. San Francisco: Chronicle Books, 1989.

Larimer, Tim. "The Ultimate Game Freak." *Time* magazine, vol. 154, no. 21, November 22, 1999.

Lee, Jessica. *The History of Pokémon*. Smashwords, April 24, 2013. [smashwords.com/books/view/309641]

Lesser, Joe. *Realistic Railroading with Toy Trains*. Waukesha, WI: Greenberg Books, 1995.

Madden, John. *All Madden*. New York: HarperCollins, 1996.

Mailerich, Dallas. *Greenberg's American Toy Trains: From 1900*. Radmore, PA: Wallace-Homestead Book Co., 1990.

McClary, Andrew. *Toys with Nine Lives*. Hartford, CT: Linnet Books, 1997.

McClintock, Inez. *Toys in America*. Washington, D.C.: Public Affairs Press, 1961.

McWhirter, Norris. *Guinness Book of World Records*. New York: Bantam, 1998.

Menke, Frank. *The Encyclopedia of Sports*. New York: A. S. Barnes, 1953.

Milne, Lyndsay. *Fun Factory: Games and Toys from Household Junk*. Westport, CT: Reader's Digest Kids, 1995.

Panati, Charles. *The Browser's Book of Beginnings*. New York: Houghton Mifflin, 1984.

Parker, Donald. *Table Tennis*. London: Blandford Books, 1993.

Pudney, John. *The Trampoline*. London: Joseph Publishing, 1959.

Raby, Mark. "Pokémon Trading Cards Getting a Free Browser-Based Game." *GamesRadar*, February 16, 2011.

Sheff, David. *Video Games*. New York: Random House, 1994.

Shinn, Gini. "Case Study: First Generation Pokémon Games for Nintendo Game Boy." Stanford University Press, Stanford University (California), March 16, 2004.

Sutton, Caroline. *How Do They Do That?* New York: William Morrow, 1981.

Theismann, Joe. *The Complete Idiot's Guide to Understanding Football Like a Pro*. New York: Simon & Schuster/Macmillan, 1997.

This Fabulous Century: 1910–1990. New York: Time-Life, 1991.

Wiswell, Tom. *America's Best Checkers*. New York: David McKay, 1957.

Yolen, Jane. *World on a String: The Story of Kites*. Cleveland: World Publishing, 1969.

WEB SITES

poof-slinky.com

aboutus.lego.com/en-us/lego-group/the_lego_history

hasbro.com

houseofplayingcards.com/playing-card-history

history1900s.about.com/od/1950s/a/sillyputty.htm

raggedyann-museum.org

ewtech.com/gijoe

planetxmagazine.com/seamonkeys

wham-o.com

angelfire.com/az2/gamesgoneby/desi4

trivialpursuit.com

americangirl.com

collectdolls.about.com/library/weekly/aa032799.htm

collectdolls.about.com/od/dollprofiles/p/americangirls.htm

ctdollartists.com/history.htm

curtdanhauser.com/AG_Collecting/Main

inventors.about.com/od/bstartinventions/a/The-History-Of-Barbie-Dolls_2.htm

hotwheels.com

answers.com/Q/How_were_hot_wheels_invented

bulbapedia.bulbagarden.net

gamesradar.com/pockets-and-monsters-history-pokemon-games

wordplays.com/help/history-of-scrabble

exploratorium.edu/skateboarding

skatelog.com/skateboarding/skateboarding-history.htm

tonyhawk.com

wiffle.com

wiffleballusa.com/history

mentalfloss.com/article/24609/it-curves-brief-history-wiffle-ball

drtoy.com/toy-history/